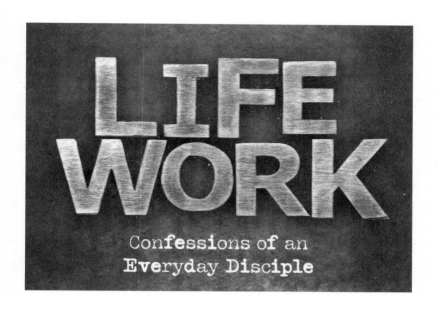

RANDY HARRIS

LEAFWOOD
PUBLISHERS

LIFE WORK

CONFESSIONS OF AN EVERYDAY DISCIPLE

LEAFWOOD
PUBLISHERS

Copyright 2014 by Randy Harris

ISBN 978-0-89112-459-7

Printed in the United States of America

Cover design by Marc Whitaker, MTW Design
Interior text design by Sandy Armstrong, Strong Design

Leafwood Publishers
1626 Campus Court
Abilene, Texas 79601
1-877-816-4455 toll free

For current information about all Leafwood titles, visit our Web site:
www.leafwoodpublishers.com

14 15 16 17 18 19 / 7 6 5 4 3 2 1

To Larry and Monty,
who know everything about me, and still love me.

ACKNOWLEDGMENTS

These chapters originated as lectures given over a number of years in many locations. We have attempted to retain the oral style in writing to keep my voice without it being annoying. Gary Holloway spent many hours working to achieve this effect and without his efforts no book would exist. The ideas, for better or worse, are mine. My graduate assistant, Travis Roberts, worked hard to improve the manuscripts, as did Leonard Allen of Leafwood Publishers.

When I look back on what I have said about being a follower of Jesus over the years, it is clear I didn't say it well enough, and, more disturbingly, was not able to fully live into what I said.

It is ever true, "Grace, Grace, all is Grace."

CONTENTS

INTRODUCTION

This is a book about ethics, usually defined as something like ideas on good and bad behavior. The ideas here come from my experience as a teacher of ethics, from reading a lot of books, and from being in a different church almost every week.

Ethics. Aren't you excited?

But you should be, because ethics are about life. They are all about living life well (hence the name of this book—*Life Work*). In these chapters I will lay out some ethical dilemmas, which will lead to a discussion of ethical theories. But do not worry, I will then get very practical and make the case for certain behaviors that would lead to a minimally decent society. And wouldn't that make for a happy change!

But this book is not an exercise in philosophical ethics. I am above all a follower of Jesus Christ. As such, the important question for us is, "How can I better follow the one whose life was all about going to a cross?" So I will make the case for cruciformity as the way of Jesus. That is, he calls us to a life of self-surrender and death for the sake of others.

Taking up the cross is a tall order. It can't be done by just trying harder. So I'm going to give you certain attitudes and practices that God can use to make you a more mature follower of Jesus. Then I want to share some things I've learned from dead and living Christians about living the cross-shaped life.

Finally, I will address the source and practices of peace—both personal, inner peace and peace between people, tribes, and nations.

For those who have read my previous books—*God Work* and *Soul Work*—some of the stories and themes here will sound familiar. Together these books kind of make up my post-systematic theology. My prayer is that God will bless you through these thoughts.

Chapter 1

TWO WAYS OF TELLING RIGHT FROM WRONG

I'm going to argue that there is a particular way of doing ethics from Scripture that makes sense. But it's going to be quite a trip. I'm not going to jump to that. I need to get you thinking about some things first.

My favorite sports headline of all time is this one: Harvard beats Yale 29–29. It's a true headline. Great headline, and therein hangs a tale. Harvard is playing Yale and everybody knows that this is *the* game. No other game matters if you're from Harvard or Yale, and so they are playing for the Ivy League championship and Yale is undefeated, and Yale is ahead in the game 29 to 13 with less than a minute to go. Harvard scores an unlikely touchdown, goes for two and makes it and now there's like forty seconds left in the game. They kick the onside kick, recover it, score a touchdown on the last play of the game and while students are pouring onto the field, they score the two point conversion to tie the game 29 to 29, so the next day in the newspaper the Harvard paper reads, Harvard beats Yale 29 to 29.

Which also tells you a great deal about human psychology, because many people at Yale still describe that as the worst day in their lives. First of all, they need to get a life. For the people at Harvard this is one of their proudest moments. But the interesting thing is . . . it's a tie. They should feel exactly the same way about it, but they don't because it's not just the destination, it's the trip. It's how you get there. So the way we are going to get where we are going is going to be a lot more interesting than the destination.

Fat Freddy

What I'm going to do is hit you with one ethical dilemma after another. Some of these are going to be totally absurd. Some of them are going to be a little more real to life, but if you take the trip with me, there's actually a point somewhere in our future. All of these are in the literature of philosophical ethics, and if you want to see their original form and lots of talk about them, they are just a Google away!

Dilemma number one. You and a group of your friends decide to go spelunking (cave exploring) in a cave down by the seaside. You stay longer than you should, and when you get ready to leave you find out that the entrance that you had come into is now underwater because the tide has come in. There is no way for you to get out. So you start exploring the cave further and find another exit, although it's not quite as big as the one you came in. There are ten of you, and leading your party is a young man that we shall describe as Fat Freddy. And Fat Freddy tries to lead first and manages to get himself stuck in the hole. And so his head and his shoulders are on the outside, but the rest of him is stuck in the cave. And the cave is filling up with water and you cannot for the life of you move Fat Freddy out of the hole. It looks as if nine of you are going to drown and the only person who will be saved is Fat Freddy since his head is on the outside.

Now you are a resourceful bunch of spelunkers and so you have brought everything you might possibly need, including one piece of dynamite which, strategically located, will remove Fat Freddy from the hole. Now this is going to be a little hard on Freddy; but if you don't do that, you're going to have nine dead people and one live one. So the question is, "Are you going to blow Fat Freddy out of the hole?"

The Dead Millionaire

By the way, I need to tell you: an ethicist never tells a happy story. If you're waiting for the happy stories, just forget it. There aren't any. Dilemma two. You go hiking with an eccentric millionaire, and as you're hiking he loses his step and falls a hundred feet down the cliff. You rush down to his side and it is clear that he's dying. He grabs your arm and says, "You know, I have never trusted banks. I have a million dollars in the backyard under the old oak tree. Would you please be sure that my son gets it?" And you say, "Sure." And he says, "No, no. Promise me that you'll see that my son gets it." And you say, "I promise." And he dies.

Now you happen to know this guy's son. You know that he is what, in ethical terms, we would describe as pond scum. You know that he is a worthless ne'er-do-well and you know that if you give him that million dollars he is just going to squander it in what Scripture might call riotous living. And no one in the world knows about the promise you've made besides you. So what you are thinking is something like this: I could say, "With his dying breath this man committed to giving $100,000 to Aids research in Africa, $100,000 to relief of the poor in Appalachia, and $100,000 to the church." And you just think of these ten places that could use $100,000. No one in the world will ever know that he didn't say that. How many of you would say I'm going to give that million dollars to his lout of a son?

Torture the Terrorist?

We are now going to do what has affectionately come to be called the 24 dilemma. How many of you have watched the television program "24"? I don't watch television, so I don't know very much about it. But they tell me this is the dilemma in every episode of "24," but I can't attest to that. There is a terrorist who has planted a dirty bomb and it is going to kill 100,000 people. We need to know where this bomb is and we don't know so our best shot at it is to try to torture this guy and get him to tell us. Otherwise, 100,000 people are going to die.

Would you torture him? How about this? He turns out to be a really tough nut to crack and it just so happens we get our hands on his seven-year-old son. How many of you would be willing to torture his seven-year-old son in front of him to get the information from the terrorist?

The Trolley Driver and the Doctor

All right, let's try just a couple more here. The famous trolley driver dilemma. You're a trolley driver (as if we knew what a trolley was). Let's make it a train. And you notice that there are three children playing down the track and if you do nothing it appears that the trolley is going to run into them and kill them. By flipping the switch you can turn the trolley onto another track where seven workers are working and you will almost certainly kill them if you turn the trolley. If you do nothing, the children will be killed. If you take action you will be directly responsible for making the choice that causes the death of seven others. How many of you say you would turn the trolley?

You are a physician and you have a patient who is a Jehovah's Witness. The parents come to you with their son who is seriously ill. He's twelve years old and without blood transfusions he's going to die. And the parents say you can treat the boy but you cannot transfuse him. Jehovah's Witnesses believe that, based on an obscure Old Testament passage, that transfusion is blood mixing, which would result in the boy going to hell. So they refuse to give permission for the transfusion. The boy also says he doesn't want the transfusion. He's only twelve. You're uncomfortable with that. You know you can save this boy's life and if you do not take action he is going to die. So, you go to court and try to get an injunction; you bring it before the judge and you say that you have to have a decision now. "This boy is going to die without a transfusion. I want you to order the transfusion so I can save this boy's life." If you're the judge are you going to order this transfusion over the boy's and parent's objection, or are you going to abide by their decision which means certain death for the young man?

The Lying Son[1]

You have an eighteen-year-old son (so you're already in a world of hurt!). You are people of very modest means. You're part of the working poor and your son is an excellent student and he wants more than anything else to go to Harvard. He's come to you and said I need $500 so I can take this college preparatory test so I can get high enough scores to go to Harvard. And you say, "Son, I'd love to do that for you, but we just don't have the money. You're just going to have to make it on your own." So he takes the test and he makes really good scores. Harvard level scores. And he comes to you and says, "I got to get this off my chest. I cheated on my college boards. I picked up a little scheme. We got the test questions before the test and I've worked really hard my whole life. I've always wanted to go to Harvard. I think I deserve to go to Harvard. You couldn't afford to help me take the preparatory test and it's kind of eating at me. I just wanted you to know that."

You're a little bothered by that. How many of you would be a little bothered by that? Now you have a tough decision to make. You might say, "Son, I don't really think you ought to go to Harvard on those scores" and he says, "Well, Dad, Mom, I'm going to. I've never done anything like this my entire life and once I get to Harvard I'll either make it on my own or I won't, but surely you're going to allow me this one indiscretion, after all it's a harmless crime. It's not like axe murder of a baby or something."

So here's my question. Are you going to allow him to go to school on those scores or are you going to say, "You are not going to school on those scores, and if I have to, I'll turn you in."

---

[1] This problem was examined in the PBS "Ethics in America" series

The Jewish Neighbor

I have one more dilemma. The Nazis come knocking on your door. You're hiding your Jewish neighbor behind the refrigerator. They say, "Do you know where your neighbor is?" Your choices are this: you either say, "No, I have no idea" or "Yes, he's behind the refrigerator, let me get him for you."

When you consider your answers to these dilemmas, I expect you will find some inconsistency. I want to explore that inconsistency to see how we think about right and wrong. And then I'm going to work my way to what I hope is a biblical position.

I never know exactly how much people know about ethics and so I'm going to pretend you don't know very much. If it turns out to be insulting, I apologize in advance. This is kind of the way ethics works. We all start out with some sort of worldview. If you are both a theist and a Christian, you are greatly influenced in your ethical reflection by that fact. As you're thinking through each of these dilemmas, you're thinking from the point of view of your Christian worldview. My guess is the reason you don't feel right about lying about the million dollars has a lot to do with your Christian worldview, because otherwise I can't see why else you would be so hesitant about that.

Worldviews and Ethical Theories

So it's your worldview that creates some sort of ethical theory and ethical theory provides a framework by which you figure things out. Now, most people's ethical theory is not very reflective and probably the reason you had some inconsistencies in your responses is that you were changing ethical theories from case to case. That's not necessarily a bad thing, but it probably is. Those ethical theories give you certain principles and it is those principles that you use to solve ethical dilemmas.

From my experience with live audiences, I've been tempted to think that absolute honesty is a central principle since many wouldn't break that promise about the money; but then many people have told me they would lie to the Nazis. So it's clear that most Christians don't mind lying from time to time. You just have to have a sufficiently good reason to do it.

Those principles lead to rules and the only difference between principles and rules is that there are a lot more rules than there are principles. In fact, before we're done I'm going to argue that there are seven principles. Seven—imagine that! There are hundreds of rules. And I'm not going to spend much time talking about rules. I'm going to talk a lot about theories and principles and then finally apply them to actions. That is, we decide what we're actually going to do.

Now take these four basic levels: worldview, ethical theory, principles/rules, and questions. One of the interesting things is you can have disagreements about any of those levels and if you're going to have an ethical discussion with somebody or an ethical argument, one of the things that often happens is people will be arguing at different levels and not know they're doing that. I can actually have pretty good ethical discussions with many atheists but we don't spend much time talking about worldview. Because sometimes we agree on principles even though we don't agree on the basic worldview. And sometimes we don't, but at least we're talking at the same level.

For a little while I want to address the level of theory. I'm not going to talk about worldview because I'm starting with the assumption that you're working out of a Christian worldview. And I will warn you, this is going to be get a little bit complicated—but you're probably reading this because there wasn't enough complication in your life.

Utilitarianism: Doing the Most Good

There are four major ethical theories—four major ways of thinking through ethics. The most prominent one is what we call *utilitarianism*. It is a teleological theory. A teleological theory is one where the rightness or wrongness of an act is determined by its outcome. The only thing we're concerned about is outcomes. Utilitarianism, as a teleological theory, wants a certain kind of outcome: it wants the most good for the most people. The rightness or wrongness of an act is determined by its outcome and the outcome the utilitarian wants is the most good for the most people.

It should be pretty obvious that that's not a bad idea. But if you work in a utilitarian way, let's run back through two or three of those dilemmas. If you're a utilitarian, what are you going to do with Fat Freddy? Blow him up! Because having nine live people and one dead one is clearly superior to having one live one and nine dead. Right?

If you're utilitarian, what are you going to do in the case of the eccentric millionaire? You're going to lie about the money, right? Because that will produce the most good for the most people and, in fact, it really doesn't have a down side in regard to the outcomes. And when it comes to torturing the terrorist, you very quickly kicked in to a utilitarian mode and said that having one terrorist in pain is clearly not as bad an outcome as having 100,000 dead people. You basically solved that in a utilitarian way. But then when I brought his son into it, many of you probably jumped—except for the three or four people who said they would torture the son too. They were being consistent with their utilitarian views because having one kid who is uncomfortable for a time as opposed to having 100,000 dead people is clearly a superior outcome. But there was something about that that I expect hit most of you wrong. When it really came down to it, you couldn't quite do that one strictly in utilitarian calculations. And when it came to that eccentric millionaire, you also couldn't just do that on utilitarian calculations. You knew the best thing to do for a good outcome would be to break the promise, but there was something in you that said, "I don't know if I should break that promise or not."

Let me make this a little bit more complex. There is the old story about the utilitarian doctor. He has three patients who all need organ transplants. You come into his office with the sniffles. All you need is an antibiotic, but it just so happens that you have organs that are compatible with the three dying patients. The doctor thinks to himself, "Well, the organs that I need, you need too, but if I did something that shortened your life, like kill you, and distributed your organs to my other patients, I would have three live ones and one dead one. As it is, I'm going to have one live one and three dead ones."

Now, here comes the crucial question. How many of you would go to that doctor? Not for the sniffles! That's right. That's exactly right. It's a great point. So what I've been describing up to this point is what we describe as *act* utilitarianism. That means you take the utilitarian principle—the most good for the most people—and you apply it directly to the act you're considering. Now if you had a doctor who acted that way you wouldn't go to that doctor. Neither would anybody else. And if people quit going to doctors, guess what? Everybody's general health declines and what we wanted was the most good for the most people, but we're not getting the most good for the most people anymore because now everybody is getting ill because they're afraid that their doctor has got three patients who need transplants in the back room.

So what we do is develop what we call *rule* utilitarianism. That is, we develop a series of rules which we then apply to the particular actions rather than applying the utilitarian principle directly to the actions. So let me try that one more time. We make a utilitarian rule that says: doctors should not kill healthy patients in order to give their organs to diseased ones. That's a good rule, right? Because that rule leads to the most good for the most people.

All right, so we're still utilitarians because we're still concerned with the outcomes—the most good for the most people—but now we're using rules rather than just applying it directly to the acts. Now, if that business of lying or breaking the promises hits you wrong, then one of the things we have to do is ask why. Why does breaking this promise—even though giving the money to other people would produce the most good for the most people—hit you wrong?

Deontology: Right Is Right

To get at that, let's consider a second major theory—what we call *deontology*. Now this is another really impressive word. It comes from a Greek word that means duty. You have certain duties. And so let me give you a really easy definition of deontology: some acts are right or wrong regardless of their consequences. What happened for most of you as you considered these dilemmas is at some points you were thinking like a utilitarian and at other points like a deontologist. That's why you are unwilling to torture the terrorist's son. It's because you decided in your mind that, even though the consequences of not doing that are horrendous, there's something wrong with the act itself. Which is, by the way, why you should have come to exactly the same conclusion in regard to the terrorist himself. You know, you can't have it both ways on that one. You've either got to torture them both or torture neither. Anything else is absolutely inconsistent. If you're making your decisions on deontological grounds, it's equally wrong in both cases. And if you're making your decisions on utilitarian grounds, it's equally justifiable in both cases, because it produces the most good for the most people.

Let me come into the real world. One of the most famous psychological experiments of the late twentieth century is now referred to just as the Milgram experiment. Stanley Milgram came up with a brilliant series of experiments. I'm going to set it up for you really quickly and then if you want to actually see some video on it you can go online and find it.

Milgram was interested in what we have come to refer to as the Nazi guard syndrome. One of the things that we're really bothered about is how perfectly good Christian people could do dreadful things simply because some authority figure tells them to. Milgram wondered if that was just a blip or if we were all susceptible to that kind of pressure, so he created the following brilliant experiment. He's got this teacher and a learner and they're sitting at a table with a partition between them, the learner on one side and the teacher on the other. He tells the learner the experiment is about the effect of negative reinforcement on learning. That is, does punishment help people learn? Now, all of you who are parents, teachers, or coaches or anything like that have at some point made a decision about whether you think negative reinforcement helps people learn. The experiment is set up so that the learner is given some information to learn and every time the learner makes a mistake the teacher pushes a button which gives the learner a mild electric shock.

The teacher has a console where every time the learner misses he or she can give an increasingly stronger shock.

Now, there is really only one subject in this experiment and it's the teacher. The learner is an actor. The learner is sitting behind the petition and will do nothing but act. Milgram is interested in how far the teacher will go. They start the experiment. The learner gets most of them right for a while then starts missing some, then starts yelping at the shocks, then starts complaining of heart trouble, then starts saying, "You're killing me!" then quits responding at all, which means he or she has either passed out or is dead. The teacher (this is all on film, by the way) is sweating bullets, becoming very distressed, and keeps looking over at the person in a lab coat who's sitting there and says, "I think he's had enough. I think we better stop the experiment." And the person in the lab coat never says anything more than this: "Teacher, please continue. We need to finish the experiment." He wanted to see how far people would go. The fact of the matter is that most teachers never stopped shocking the students, which is very sobering.

Now I'm just wondering. We found out some really important information. Nobody was really hurt, though some people were distressed. How many of you would say you find that experiment unethical? How many would say you think that it is fine? The way you answer that is largely determined by whether you're a utilitarian or a deontologist. If you are a deontologist, you say that you don't treat people like that. You don't have a right to treat a person like a lab rat, which is essentially what you're doing here. If you're a utilitarian you say the outcomes were very important and we discovered some really important information. Nobody was really hurt. It was no big deal.

Now let me see if I can again make it a little bit more complex. Most of you will be aware of the famous incident in one of the wars. I don't remember if it was Korea or World War II. You have soldiers who are in great pain and you've run out of morphine, and so what the doctors did was to say, "I'm going to give you some morphine. You know this is really strong stuff. I can't give you too much." But he's giving him nothing. He's got nothing to give him. And he is going to lie as convincingly as he can, trying to convince this soldier he's given him morphine.

What we found is that the placebo effect is very profound. About 60 percent of the soldiers they treated with nothing got relief because they sold the idea it was morphine. They lied through their teeth, lied convincingly over and over. Even when they had to come back a second time, they said, "Look, I can only give you a little bit more. If I give you much more of this I'm going to be in danger of killing you with the morphine." That kind of lying.

How many of you would say that's right? Most of you, I expect. So one of the questions we have to ask is, Are we now utilitarians? Did I just decide that outcomes are the most important thing or is there some other way to think about this?

Chapter Two

TWO MORE WAYS OF TELLING RIGHT FROM WRONG

In the last chapter we looked at utilitarianism and deontology as two ethical theories, two ways of telling right from wrong. Another ethical theory is *relativism*, and some of you are acting as relativists as you respond to our dilemmas. It's a little hard to do that out of the Christian worldview, but some people do.

Relativism: What Is Right for You

A relativist basically says the following: whatever Mary thinks is right or wrong is right or wrong for Mary. There are no objective principles. Every person decides what they think is the right thing to do in any particular situation. Relativists just work from situation to situation; whatever they think is right in a particular situation is what they go with—we really don't have any other way of judging than that.

One of the great relativists of the late twentieth century was John Paul Sartre, a French philosopher and an atheist. He says that when God disappears objective morals disappear too. He explained it something like the following:

If I draw a single line on a marker board and ask, "Which line is longer?" how would you answer? Sartre says that trying to do morals without God is like asking which line is longer. There's nothing to compare it to, so it doesn't make any sense to even ask the question. There's no way to know whether anything's right or wrong. Basically all you can appeal to are the standards of your society.

I like to mess with my students on this one. A lot of my students are what I would call sloppy relativists. They're not even good relativists. I'll give them the following old dilemma. You're a missionary. You go into an area in Africa that's pretty far back in the bush and polygamy is still the way the whole culture operates. If you go in there and break up the polygamist marriages, you are going to put orphans on the streets. You're going to destroy the whole social structure. You're going to create orphans and women who have no way to support themselves. Would you go in there and break up those polygamist marriages?

I always have students who will say, "Well, you have to break up those polygamous marriages." I say, "Why?" They say, "Well, because polygamy is a sin." I say, "How do you know that?" And they say, "The Bible." I say, "Show me that verse." And then we go looking for the verse. And that takes quite a hunt. Eventually one student raises his hand and says, "I found it." Now I'm shocked because I couldn't find it and I say, "What is it?" and he says, "No man can serve two masters." I say, "I appreciate that, but I think that passage has a context and I don't think that's it."

There's a problem in taking the values of your society and placing them on top of some other society, and kind of becoming the ugly American. We think our values are superior to everybody else's values. Relativists point to that.

Why Relativism Is Bad

I want to say two or three really quick things about relativism because I think it's a really bad idea. If relativism is really true then there is no action that you can say is wrong in and of itself. The major professor I studied with at Syracuse University was a complete moral relativist. He did not believe in God. He did not believe in truth. He did not believe in family. He was a divorced, alcoholic, lapsed Mormon atheist who had been basically run out of a liberal denomination. Not easy to do. He was the most consistent moral relativist I've ever known. But to be a moral relativist what you have to say is that, if your kid comes to my house at Halloween and I decide to give him rat poison instead of candy, there is no objective moral difference in those things. Now you can put me in jail for it because society thinks it's a bad idea, but you can't say it's wrong. You can't say anything is wrong.

Whenever I have somebody who takes that point of view, I usually just reach out and slap them. The question is, can you live in that kind of world? And a lot of relativists point out that people do in fact have different ideas about what's right and wrong. We just proved that a little earlier, right? But the fact that we disagreed about that doesn't mean there is no right or wrong. It just means some of us might be better or worse ethicists than others. That is, I might give you a really complicated math problem and some of you would get it right and some of you would get it wrong; but the fact that we got several different answers didn't mean there was no right answer. It just means some of us aren't as good at math as others. It also means if you're a complete moral relativist then you think that the only standards are the standards of society and that all moral reformers are always immoral because the only standard for what's right is what society believes is right.

Intuitively we know that's not true. But if you're a complete moral relativist it has to be true. I have not known very many people who could live with that. They say it when it's convenient, when they want to do what they want to do. But when I have students who claim to be complete moral relativists and I announce a test for one time and then decide to give it the day before, they quit being moral relativists immediately. They say, "You know, you're being unfair." "On what basis? I think this is cool," I respond. And since I'm the one who decides, that's pretty hard to live with. They may think I've lied to them, but when you're a relativist, lying is okay. (And, by the way, many of you just decided you were going to lie to the Nazis, so I'm not hanging out here all by myself.)

I'm now going to hit you with my favorite dilemma of all time. It's best for students but the rest of you will understand it. I call this the Moby Dick dilemma. It is your last semester in college. You are getting ready to graduate with a degree in accounting. You have a job lined up with one of the few big accounting firms that are still left. You have this girl or boy who is going to marry you. Life is perfect. And then you get the dreaded call from the registrar's office. You are one course short of graduation. You cry. You complain. You try to negotiate, but if you don't know this you should: it is easier to negotiate with a terrorist than it is with the registrar. Finally you give in and ask, "What do I have to do?"

You have to take an English course. And so you take the only English course that works into your schedule which is Early American Literature. The first thing that you read in this course is *The Scarlet Letter*. There's a good chance you read this book in school. As you know, it is a fascinating book. It is all about sex but still manages to be boring. Leave it to the Puritans to take the most salacious possible topics and make them boring. You get through that loser and then you read *Huckleberry Finn* and you're delighted about that because you didn't know that was literature. After that you get to the poetry. None of it rhymes. But the great thing about poetry is its short. You're doing fine. You then come to the last assignment in the course which is to read the great American novel which everyone knows is *Moby Dick*.

I'm now going to ask how many of you have read Moby Dick. And I'm not asking how many of you were assigned it. How many of you have read it? For those of you who haven't, *Moby Dick* is eight hundred dense pages about whaling. You're from Kansas. Whales have not been an important part of your life. You're guessing they're not going to be. By the way, my favorite abridgment of *Moby Dick* consists of one sentence. "Everyone dies but Ish and fish." That is really all you need to know. And you think, "I've been a good sport up until now, but I'm not reading *Moby*

Dick." You read the *SparkNotes* (Cliff for a new generation) because you figure whoever wrote those things is going to understand the book better than you would have anyway. But you don't stop there because you're a good student. You watch both movies. The one with Gregory Peck and the one with the Star Trek guy. And by the way, the Gregory Peck one is better. Way better. Amen.

Well, you're not expecting to make an A on this test. You're just trying to get a C and get on with your life. You get to the final test and this idiot of a professor has put only one question on the final test. Worth one hundred points. Did you read Moby Dick? And out in parentheses he has "the movies and the *SparkNotes* don't count." And if you answer this truthfully you will get zero points on the final. You will fail the course. You won't graduate. You will lose the job you have lined up and that girl or boy is probably not going to marry a loser like you. Would you tell the truth in that circumstance?

Now it's interesting when I present this to my students. Some students who I didn't think could think at all suddenly become theologians. "Let's see. God is timeless so I can say I read the book. I will read it later, and it'll be the same to God!" I have given this dilemma to my ethics classes for a decade now at Abilene Christian University and you will be interested to know that 95 percent of my students say in that case of course they would lie. I strongly suspect that the other 5 percent are lying about the fact that they wouldn't. Not only do they tell me they would lie in that case, they then proceed to try to convince me why that would be the right thing to do. Melville's dead. It's a victimless crime. God wants them to marry this girl and get this job so they'll be able to contribute to the church.

Virtue Ethics:
The Kind of Person You Are

Now the reason I give that dilemma to my students is because my students are death on public figures who get caught in a difficult situation and then keep lying until it's no longer plausible. And what I want them to see is that, if the consequences are high enough, most people's integrity is for sale. And if you don't lie in that situation I'd contend there's only one reason that you don't. *Because you're not that kind of person.* This is another form of ethics which we call virtue ethics, which is not really about what kind of actions we do, but about what kind of people we are.

But if you do any kind of cost benefit analysis on the dilemma I just gave you, you're going to lie. The only reason you wouldn't lie is because that's just not the kind of person you are.

I've got to tell you, I think virtue ethics takes care of a large percentage of the moral life. We act out of who we are as people. But virtue ethics doesn't help you solve any of those dilemmas I gave earlier. Virtue ethics is terrible on dilemmas. It's good on ordinary life, so let me briefly address what a real ethical dilemma is. The way we think about ethical dilemmas is generally not right. Ethical dilemmas are situations where you cannot decide what the right thing to do is. And that makes up a very small percentage of the moral life. Most of our moral life is spent deciding whether we are going to do what we know is the right thing to do.

Can you see the difference? In one case I know what the right thing to do is. It just may be that there is some cost involved in it and I don't know if I'm going to do it or not. In other cases we are genuinely baffled about what the right thing to do is.

I'm getting ready to tell you a true story and I'm going to have to disguise it a little. Ethics requires that. It's important that you know the story is true, though many of the details have been changed. I have had several such conversations and could not tell you the name of the persons involved if I wanted to do so. These kind of things go on everyday in our current medical world. I was speaking on ethics on one occasion and I used a lot of the material that I'm writing about here. There were a lot of laughs. We had some fun. I think we made a little headway. A person came up afterwards and said she had an ethics question. I could see that she was a little teary and I said sit down. She had a person with her that I later learned was her husband.

She said, "My son had a disease. And it ravaged his body and he was so young. His heart was so strong he wouldn't die." And one of the physicians said to me, "Tell me when you're ready and we'll end this." She says, "I'm ready. " So the doctor basically overdosed the son on painkillers. At that stage of life you're on the edge anyway and so it's not that hard to do. And she says to me, "Now what I want to know is did I kill my son? Was God trying to teach us something? I want to know if I killed my son. I want to know if what I did was unethical."

Now that's a genuine moral dilemma. You know, this is not like my students trying to decide what they're going to do with their boyfriend or girlfriend in the car. They very well know what the right thing to do is. They're just trying to decide whether they're going to do it or not. This is where you're wrestling with your soul. Trying to figure out what the right thing to do is. Virtue ethics are very good at telling you what to do in the back seat of a car. They're not very good at solving the problem of what to do with this person who is in terrible pain. Good for most of life. Not so good for dilemmas. And almost everyone is going to have end of life dilemmas with family members.

Respect for Persons

Now I'm getting ready to argue a case. It's not going to be convincing to all of you, but I hope that as I argue my case you'll become clearer and clearer about your own ethical viewpoint. My ethical stance is what would be described as a pluralistic deontologist. As a deontologist I think that there are some actions that are right or wrong regardless of their consequences. That you have certain duties. As a *pluralistic* deontologist I think there are several duties. In fact, I believe there are exactly seven of them. And the reason that I have ethical dilemmas is because sometimes my seven duties come in conflict with each other. So when the Nazis come and ask about my Jewish neighbor, I have a duty to tell the truth—but I also have a duty to do no harm. And I have to decide which of those duties is going to trump the other one. I experience tension because these duties are going in different directions.

Now, I'm actually going to argue that pluralistic deontology is the biblical way. We'll see if this works. I'm going to try to ground it in Scripture. I think that the ethic that Scripture tries to get off the ground is what I might call a respect of persons ethic.

So let me first address what it means to respect a person. There are two different kinds of respect I can give you. One kind of respect I can give you is based on your achievements. You may have achieved something superb in sports or in music or in academics and I respect your accomplishments. The other kind of respect I can give you is based simply on your being a creature in the image and likeness of God. And I give that respect to every human being. That's the kind of respect I'm going to talk about. It's important not to get these two types confused.

It's really interesting when I get my teacher evaluations back. I've got this D- student who tells me, "You didn't teach me anything." And I'm thinking, "Well, I told you that first. That's the one thing we agree on." That D- student deserves the same respect for being created in the image and likeness of God as the A student does. They deserve exactly the same amount and the same kind of respect. That's hard. Because we're trained in a culture to believe that the only kind of respect that matters is the respect that you get because of certain achievements. (And by the way, those achievements have a whole lot less to do with you than you think they do anyway.)

I want to talk about this more in the next chapter, because I think a respect of persons ethic can provide a minimally decent ethic for our whole society. Scripture spends a good bit of time trying to explain to us what it means to respect a person that way, and I'm going to give you what I think are the seven principles that emerge out of Scripture. I also want to argue that most people who don't believe in the Bible believe in these seven principles. I believe that you can teach ethics in public schools and never mention God or the Bible and that if we would start teaching these seven principles we would have a much better world than we currently live in.

This is not going to be a Good Samaritan ethic. I will address Good Samaritanism later. What I will lay out here is a minimally decent Samaritan ethic. I don't know if you've noticed, but we are a far cry from reaching the level of minimally decent in our culture. I'm not going to stop with the minimally decent, but I do want to present the basic elements of such an ethic.

Chapter Three

FOUR PRINCIPLES OF A MINIMALLY DECENT ETHIC

T he respect of persons made in the image of God can provide a minimally decent ethic for our society, even for those who do not believe the Bible. Having said that, I believe these seven principles are found in Scripture. We'll look at the first four principles in this chapter and the last three in the next chapter. This pluralistic deontology approach emphasizing multiple duties is mostly indebted to W. D. Ross, who has his own list of what he calls prima facie (on the face of it) duties. His list is not identical to mine, but the origins of these ideas are his.

Do No Harm

Number one: non-malfeasance. This means to do no harm. The first principle is to try as best I can not to harm people. The vast majority of the Ten Commandments are expressions of non-malfeasance. Do not steal. Do not commit adultery. Do not kill. It's the simplest and most basic duty. If I'm driving to school and I'm running a little late and I see one of my students has had a flat tire, I may not be obligated to stop and help him change it, but the least I can do is not to swerve and pick him off. Do no harm. In a world as complex and closely knit together as ours, you have to pay more attention to do no harm than you used to. I've got to pay attention to what kind of shoes I buy because the kind of shoes I buy may be actively doing harm to somebody. I've got to think about how the coffee I drink gets on the table. This do no harm is a deep principle. It means psychological harm, social harm, and physical harm. It means that as far as possible I'm going to try to live a life where I'm not actively harming people. Our world would get better if we would simply quit hurting each other.

Do Good

Number two: beneficence. The second principle is similar to the first. Beneficence means basically to do good. But it's actually a more complex principle and will take some explaining. If this principle were exactly like the first one, you would have had to do good to everybody that you meet on your way to anywhere, and you would never get anywhere. So doing good is not as strong an obligation as not doing harm. The philosophical notion of beneficence is based on two things: the cost to me and the benefit to the other.

Now remember, I'm going to describe a minimally decent Samaritan here. These two things are inversely related. The lower the cost to me, the higher the benefit to the other—and the greater the obligation. Easy illustrations. Some of you are old enough to remember when the Air Florida plane took off from National Airport in Washington DC, hit the bridge over the Potomac River, and plunged into the icy river. Do you remember those gripping pictures of the helicopter dropping down the rescue hook and the one guy who kept handing the hook to other people and eventually died? Let us suppose that I'm standing on the bank of the Potomac River that day and I'm not a particularly good swimmer. My idea of swimming is trying not to drown. And I see those people flopping around out there in that icy river. Do I have the moral obligation to jump in and try to swim out and save one? I would argue that that would be a very laudatory thing for me to do, but that you really wouldn't consider me morally reprehensible if I didn't.

Let me give another example. Let us suppose I'm walking along the side of this little babbling brook and I notice that a two-year-old has stumbled and fallen in face first. He's in two feet of water. And you know how two-year-olds are. They're like turtles. He can't get up. He's drowning. Just by putting my foot in the brook I can grab him by the back of the shirt and pull him out. And I think to myself, "I don't think I want to do that. I have my good shoes on. I'll get my feet all wet." In this case, if I don't save him you're going to consider me morally reprehensible, right? Because the benefit to the other is extremely high and the cost to me is extremely low.

So the philosophical obligation is not that I have to do every single good thing that I ever have the possibility of doing—which is impossible. But it is that when the cost to me is low and the benefit to another is high, I have a moral responsibility to act.

I watch very little television and when I watch it I watch sports and news. I have not watched network TV in a long time. But I hang out with students so I know exactly what's going on. Several years ago when I found out that the last episode of Seinfeld was coming up—which I have never watched a single time—I said, "Oh, I'm going to watch the last episode because I saw the last episode of MASH and Mary Tyler Moore." When I watched I noticed something very interesting for a famous comedy. It was not in the least bit funny—but it was utterly brilliant. The writers used the last show to make fun of the whole show because what they'd always been accused of is portraying totally self-absorbed people who don't care about anybody else. So they wind up the show by getting them all arrested for breaking a Good Samaritan law. They watched somebody getting mugged. They're laughing about it but don't know that the state they're in has a Good Samaritan law. So they all get put in prison because they didn't do anything about it. I love it. Brilliant! Wasn't funny, but it was brilliant.

The law notices the difference in these two things. You know when you actively do harm and when you fail to do good; but there are some cases where the good must be done because the cost to oneself is so low and the benefit to the other is so high.

Tell the Truth

Number three: truth telling. It is true that not all lies are created equal. But I do want to notice that in Scripture the primary identity of Satan is the one who lies or deceives. Failing to be truthful, in Scripture's point of view, is really serious business. Very quickly, there are basically three different kinds of lies. First, there is the lie to harm another. That is where I tell a malicious lie in order to try to hurt somebody. Second, there is the lie to protect oneself, which is the most common lie. "The dog ate my homework. My computer won't print. The check is in the mail. That's a beautiful hat." Third, there is the lie to protect another. "Do you know where your Jewish neighbor is?" "I don't think so."

These three types of lies aren't exactly the same. If you push me to the edges, I will give you permission to lie to the Nazis about your Jewish neighbor. If you need my permission, you've got it. But I always wonder what to do when somebody comes up and shows me their baby. All babies to me look a little bit like Yoda, so I say, "Yeah, your baby is out of this world." I don't know if I'm trying to protect myself or trying to protect them. But the vast majority of lies that we tell are lies to protect ourselves. I do want to point out that we can't have any kind of relationships at all if we can't depend on the basic veracity of the person in front of us. And boy, we are in a truth telling crisis! I find it harder to tell the truth than I wish I did. I don't know if I've just sucked up too much of the culture, but truthfulness and integrity is harder than it should be. But it's pretty close to the center in Scripture because Satan is the deceiver, the father of lies.

Keep Your Promises

Number four: promise-keeping. Four is closely related to three but they're not exactly the same. In the Bible there is a heavy word attached to promise-keeping. It is the word covenant. It is one of the most important words in the Old Testament. The verb that goes with covenant is cut. You cut a covenant. Some scholars think it goes back to ancient practice that when you make a covenant with another person you hack up an animal and the two of you walk between the pieces of the hacked up animal; the symbolism is, if you break this covenant what has happened to this animal should happen to you. By the way, I have been trying to introduce that into the wedding ceremonies that I perform, but it's not really going that well. It would accomplish two things. It shows the solemnity of this covenant and it will also keep the cat population down. It's all pluses. So this business of making covenants is very important.

Now let me tell you the difference between promise keeping and truth telling. In promise keeping, because of some action I've done or thing that I've said in the past, I've created obligations for myself that I did not previously have. Let me give you an example. Let's suppose that I have somebody who needs a kidney transplant and I'm compatible and I volunteer to give one of my kidneys. I am under absolutely no obligation to do that, but I say, "I'll do that," and then as they're rolling us down to the operating room, I say, "Wait a minute, I've changed my mind!" I wouldn't have done anything immoral if I'd not agreed to it in the first place, but when I agree to it and then decide I'm not going to do it, I've done something seriously immoral.

Or take class attendance by my students. I like to teach 8 AM classes because I'm as alert then as I'm ever going to be—students not so much. They live what I would describe as a vampiric existence. They tend to rove at night and then kind of sleep through the day. On my student evaluations one of the questions is, "Does the teacher start the class on time?" I always tell my 8 AM classes, "How would you know, since I was the only one here when class started?" I say to them, "There would be something kind of silly about calling all of your roommates and friends and asking them why they don't come to class if they hadn't signed up for the class." They're under no obligation to come; but once they've signed up for the class they have an obligation they didn't have before.

That's what promise keeping is. I take an obligation on myself and then I have to keep it. So we also have a big promise-keeping problem. The primary problem is that we make way too many promises. We don't appreciate the solemnity of covenant. I'm an academic. If you ask an academic to write something and you put the date due period far enough in advance, they'll agree to anything—knowing that they're going to miss the date when they sign up for it, which is seriously immoral. It erodes the notion of promise keeping. "Are you going to be there?" "Yes." You just created an obligation for yourself you didn't have a moment before—which is one reason why the answer to that question is almost always "Maybe."

My favorite new area of intellectual inquiry is behavioral economics. I think it's some of the most insightful work being done in the academy. For years economics was based on the notion of rational consumption. Do you see anything wrong with that theory? Have you noticed that your consumption isn't entirely rational? And so these economics folks, instead of assuming that consumers are rational, have started to study the way consumers actually behave, which is far more interesting. (See the book *Predictably Irrational* by Dan Ariely for some great studies, including those I have referenced here.)

There are hundreds of great studies. One of my favorites is this one. In taste tests, do more people prefer Pepsi or Coke? The answer is: Pepsi and Coke. Depends on how you do it. In blind taste tests Pepsi wins. If people know what they're drinking, Coke wins. And in fact, when people know they're drinking Coke and they're wired up, parts of the brain light up that do not light up when they're drinking Coke and don't know what it is. What that means is Coke is not selling you a taste. Coke is selling you a story. It is no accident that the Santa Claus suit and the Coke can are exactly the same color. The St. Nicholas that you know was virtually invented by the Coca Cola Company. He used to wear all sorts of colors, but now he's all red. He's Coca Cola red. He's got a Coke in his hand. These people who are trying to sell you a story are really good at it.

Another study has people playing a computer game. By clicking on certain doors or windows they make money. But if they do not click on a certain door or window at a particular point, that door or window will disappear. What researches have seen over and over again is that people, especially young people, will click on that door or window that is about to disappear even though it is clear that it is not in their financial best interests to do so. Now for people who are trying to do church that is a profound study because it says that people place more value on keeping all of their options open rather than on commitment, which is why we have such enormous commitment problems with people under a certain age. Commitment means closing doors. They have been acculturated from the very beginning to think that they have to keep all of their options open—which is why the answer to the question, "Are you going to be there?" is almost always "Maybe."

When we start making promises, we start to slam certain doors shut because when I'm saying I'm going to be here it means I can't be there. Bringing promise-keeping or covenant-keeping back to the prominence that it deserves is going to be really hard work.

Chapter Four

THREE MORE PRINCIPLES OF A MINIMALLY DECENT ETHIC

So we do no harm, we do good, we tell the truth, and we keep promises. What other principles lead to minimal decency?

Be Fair

Number five: justice. To create the biblical groundwork for this principle, we would want to look at the whole set of the Minor Prophets, where justice is one of the primary themes. You remember Amos 5 where God says, "I hate, I despise your religious assemblies. I wish you'd knock off all that worship stuff. What I really want is this. I want justice to roll down like a river and righteousness like an everflowing stream." The emphasis is on justice and righteousness, not on worship.

I'm going to make some effort here to define justice, which is notoriously difficult. Basically what I'm thinking about when I'm thinking about justice is fairness. Harvard philosopher John Rawls is the great advocate of this idea. It means that I treat like cases alike and I treat different cases differently depending on the relevant differences. So, for instance, those of you who have children of wildly different ages, I assume you have different rules for your six-year-old and your sixteen-year-old, because that age difference is relevant and the fair thing to do is to treat them with reference to their relevant differences.

Where it becomes unjust is where we treat irrelevant differences as if they're relevant. Here's an example from Scripture. How much money you have should not have any impact on what happens to you when you go to court. That's all over the Old Testament because whether you're rich or poor is not relevant to the issue of getting a fair day in court, at least it shouldn't be. So in my ethics class, let's say, I have two students who each have exactly the same averages and exactly the same amount of absences, but I give one an A and one a C. The person who gets the C catches wind of it and comes to me and asks why he got a C, and I say, "Well, because you're blonde and I've just never cared for blondes." That's not a relevant difference and they're going to accuse me of unfairness.

Now this is harder than it looks because it's not always clear what differences are relevant; it's always easy to have a kind of straight, formal justice. My students claim they want that—except they don't. They'll say things like "We want exactly the same rules to apply to everybody," and that's true except in the cases where it applies to them. So let's say I have a student who regularly smoked marijuana with his or her parents while growing up. This student had a friend at church and started coming to church, and then had a conversion experience. He or she came to our university and was trying to work out of a really terrible lifestyle; but he or she slips up and smokes marijuana sometimes. Do I treat that in the same way I would a situation where a person is coming out of a wholly different background? What's relevant here? What's the just thing to do?

So I appreciate the complications, but I always have the goal of wanting to treat people justly or fairly. I have these conversations with my students. I say, "It's really important to me that when you walk out of here you feel as if I have treated you in a way that's fair, and if you don't think I'm treating you fairly, we need to have an ethics discussion about it. What would be a fair way to handle this?"

Respect Autonomy

Number six: respect for autonomy. Nice words. What that means is, insofar as possible, I'm going to allow you to make all the decisions for your life even when I think you're making bad decisions. I hinge this in Jesus who invited people to come follow him. Hear the word: invitation. Christianity at its best is not a religion of the sword (though we have not always been at our best). You let people decide. They make their own decisions, and for the most part I'm going to try to allow people to do that.

Now that doesn't mean people can do just anything. There are limits to autonomy, the primary limit being when your autonomy starts to interfere with somebody else's autonomy. So you are not free to kill all redheads because that interferes with the autonomy of redheads. Other than that obvious one, there are basically two limits that we usually place when we try to respect people's autonomy. They have to do with maturity and rationality. If I have a person who is clearly irrational, I am not going to show as much respect for his or her autonomy as I would for somebody who's not. For instance, if I have this guy who is on drugs and thinks he's Batman and doesn't remember that Batman can't fly and he's getting ready to jump off the building, I'm not going to say, "Well , it's his choice." No, I'm going to do everything I can to restrain him because he's not acting fully rational.

I'm almost never sick, and when I am my approach has generally been to ignore it and it will eventually go away. The sickest I've ever been was in high school when I got strep throat, which tends not to go away by itself. I ignored it, and by the time I went to the doctor I had a temperature of about 113. I've got puss hanging off my tonsils. I can't eat. I can't swallow. I'm almost delirious and they tell me somewhere along the way that I said something like, "Just shoot me." And so they said, "Well, we've got to respect the guy's autonomy. Where's the gun?" If people are not thinking clearly then you don't respect their autonomy. That's one limit.

Another limit is based on a person's maturity. If someone is not fully mature, you don't fully respect their autonomy. So when the six-year-old says, "Mommy, Mommy, can I go play on the freeway?" you say, "Hey, it's your choice. Go knock yourself out." No, you don't do that because he or she is not mature enough to make that decision yet.

Now, of course the thing that's really complicated about that is when you get to those awful late adolescent years. Now culture does make a difference here. I've been teaching a long time and we're all wrestling with what sociologists describe either as delayed adolescence or emerging adulthood, depending on which kind of spin you want to put on it. Basically what it means is this: sociologists say adolescence now ends somewhere around age twenty-six or twenty-seven. So I'm living with it and those of you who have teenagers are really living with it.

When I first started teaching I would catch persons at age twenty and usually think that I'm catching them at the end of adolescence. Now I realize I'm catching them right in the middle of it and I tend to be more bemused by this than irritated by it. When I'm more irritated by it, I'll try to quit teaching. Sometimes it's hard to be bemused; in one moment I'll get this action of incredible maturity and the next moment I'll get this incredible immaturity. I don't know from one moment to the next which one I'm going to get. That's what makes teaching undergraduates so much fun—except during final test week when it's predictable. It's immature all the way to the end.

Those of you who have teenage or college age children are probably experiencing this. There seems to be no full explanation for it. I think it's the cell phone that did this—I am only half kidding. When I grew up and was going to college, none of us had any money. We were all fairly poor. The cell phone really hadn't arrived yet and we would typically talk to our parents once a month. My students talk to their parents six or seven times a day. First thing they do when they have a problem is call home. If they have a problem with me, they call home and then sometimes their parents call me and I say some harsh things to them. Well, it's a little harder to grow up. So now I have to wrestle with when and how much autonomy I give to people who aren't fully cooked yet. You notice I avoided half baked. For instance, do you believe a sixteen-year-old ought to be able to make the decision about abortion on her own? Do you believe that a sixteen-year-old ought to be able to make a decision about whether to go through the rigors of chemotherapy or not?

Those are really hard questions, as we try to figure out how much autonomy we're going to give people. If we were together long enough, you would find that the way I do ethics is very much driven by this value. I think people have a right to make their own decisions, even if those are decisions of which I disapprove. My goal in those situations is to try to be persuasive, not coercive. Now, there are some times when I'm just coercive; where, because of the maturity of the person or the stakes, I just tell the person this is what you need to do and I'll try to compel him or her to do it if I have to. But those are going to be the exceptions. For the most part I want to respect the other person's ability to make decisions.

By the way, there is also another thing that goes with autonomy. If I'm going to respect your autonomy to make decisions, then you have to take responsibility for those decisions. Here again my friend, philosopher John Paul Sartre, says the only really unethical thing is for you not to take responsibility for your decisions. So I make a little speech to my students the first day of class. I'll say, "You want to be treated like adults, I want to treat you like adults. I will respect whatever values you decide to accept. All I'm saying is that you have to take responsibility for it. So if you come to me in the middle of the term and say, 'Hey, I have an opportunity to go to Haiti and save some children,' I will say, 'Great! I'm really glad you got that opportunity.' And they will say, 'I'm going to have to miss a couple of days of your class.' I say, 'Yes,' and they say, 'Well, I've already missed several days of your class. If I go to Haiti it's going to put me over the limit and I'll be dropped from your class. Should I go to Haiti?' 'I don't know. I think it sounds like great ministry.' 'Good, then you won't drop me from class?' 'No, I'm going to drop you from class.' 'But I have to have your class.' 'Then stay.' 'But the children are dying in Haiti.' 'Then go.' 'But I have to pass your class.' In the kindest possible way I say, 'This is not my problem and I'll respect whatever decision you make, but you decide.'"

Or you've got my 8:00 AM class and you come to me and say, "You've probably noticed that I miss your class a good bit and sometimes I'm late." And I say, "Yes, I have noticed that." "And you know you give those quizzes at the beginning of the class and my average on those is like zero because I always get there too late for the quiz." And I say, "Yea, I've noticed that." "And I thought I should explain to you why that is." And I say, "Great, I would love to hear that. I can't think of anything I'd rather do." "Well, I'm taking eighteen hours and I've got a job where I'm working thirty hours a week and I'm just beating myself to death." And I said, "Good night! Man, you've got my admiration. I don't think I could do that." "Well, I don't know if you've noticed, but I'm not doing it so well either." "Yea, I saw that." "You think I could take those quizzes at the end of class instead of the beginning?" "No, I don't think so. Let me make a better suggestion. Why don't you drop my class? You know, its Introduction to Philosophy. It's totally irrelevant anyway." "I must have this class." "Well, why don't you drop another class?" "No, I need to get through school." "Why don't you work fewer hours?" "I can't, I've got to have the money." "Do you have a car?" "Yeah." "Sell it." "I can't sell my car." I say, "What do you want me to do here? You've made a set of decisions and you now have to take responsibility for those decisions. This, in the kindest possible way, is not my problem."

We need a strong dose of respect for autonomy and what goes with it—the acceptance of responsibility. People have to start taking responsibility for the decisions they make; trying to avoid that responsibility or place it on somebody else is a sure sign of a lack of maturity and, unless I respect people's autonomy, they never do quite grow into that responsibility. And I've got some students who learned that.

Fix What You Break

Number seven: reparations. Reparations is a fancy word for "You broke it, so you fix it." That is, you make repairs. You make amends. Again, I think if you look carefully in Scripture, you'll see that's actually a fairly significant theme. That is, we make mistakes, we do bad things. Then our responsibility is in whatever way we can to try to set those things right. And that requires that we be willing to admit that we're wrong, that we caused damage, and that we need to repair it. Now the reason that I put this last is that we live in a culture where the primary point of the American judicial system is to work on the problem of reparations. Courts spend more time doing reparations than they do everything else combined. That comprises most of civil litigation.

It's going to take some space to explain the concept of reparations. Reparations depend on two things. First, it depends on who's responsible, and second, on determining the proper recompense. When I'm clearly responsible and I can repay *in kind* this becomes fairly simple.

A quick scenario. I live in Texas so I'm going to go hunting and try to kill Bambi. So I go to Farmer Jones and I say, "Farmer Jones, would it be all right if I hunt on your land?" And he says, "Sure, just be careful." So I go out to kill Bambi and I see Bambi through the trees; I fire, but it turns out this is not a deer, it is Farmer Jones' cow (which, by the way, is easier to kill; cows have a number of positive things about them, but evasive maneuvers are not their best thing). And I think, "Oh man, this is embarrassing!" But assuming that the cow was not a pet, you know this is not horrible. I go and knock on Farmers Jones' door and I say, "I shot for the deer and missed it, but killed your cow. Let me replace your cow." Simple. Straightforward. No problem.

The problems come when I cannot repay in kind, and it's easy to give examples. A hospital in Florida is supposed to amputate a guy's leg, but they make a tragic error and cut off the wrong leg. How do you pay back? How do you repair this damage? You cannot give back the leg and so there's only one way to do it—money. We have to decide what a leg is worth.

Or we could point to the celebrated Union Carbide accident in Bhopal, India where thousands and thousands of Indian workers were killed. Reparations must be made, but then you have to do the really ugly calculations, trying to figure out how much an Indian life is worth. This is sobering business. Another famous case is the McDonalds coffee case. A person drives through McDonalds, buys coffee, spills it in the lap, and then sues McDonalds for getting scalded. The court awards a huge sum which is later reduced on appeal. McDonalds, by the way, had been warned repeatedly that their coffee was too hot and ignored the warnings. The court decided to get their attention with money.

This illustration points us to a second problem with reparations: determining how far the line of responsibility extends. For instance, should a person who has a family member killed by a drunk driver be able to sue the bartender who let the person go out drunk? The people who really live in dread of these kind of lawsuits are toy makers, because there is almost no predicting what a young child will decide to do with the toy that you never intended for them to do. How responsible am I for somebody using my equipment in ways that I never expected? Most of us are, in one way or another, beneficiaries of past slave labor in the United States. The economics on this is pretty clear. So how far does the line of responsibility extend? Do you have some responsibility to make reparations for stuff that your ancestors did but for which you now have certain privileges?

Clearly, working out the details of reparations is pretty complicated. But the basic principal remains—if I broke it, I have obligations to fix it. I've got to try to straighten out my own messes.

A Minimally Decent Ethic

These seven principles, I think, provide a definition of what a minimally decent Samaritan ethic would look like. This is what I owe to every other person in the world, and it should be impossible for you to come up with some responsibility that does not fall somewhere under my seven. The only other one I've considered for a while but haven't put on the list yet is whether self-improvement is itself a moral obligation that I owe other people As you can see, it's not on the list yet, so I'm not totally convinced. But an argument can be made there.

My conviction is that these principles are all grounded in Scripture, but people who have little regard for Scripture will, for the most part, still agree with this list. They will agree that if we're going to have a world that is going to function in some reasonable way then these are the sort of things that we basically owe to one another.

Now moral dilemmas for the most part are of the following sort: we have two choices and both of them are bad choices. We generally refer to this as choosing the lesser of two evils. We do occasionally have two good choices where we're trying to choose the best of the two goods—and that's a really happy occasion

I want to kick into theologian mode for a moment. If you haven't been able to tell up to now, let me make it explicit. I think ethics is a tragic enterprise and that salvation, if it occurs, does not occur because of ethical acumen; it occurs because of the grace of God. Even when I have done my best, there's still something tragic about it. I can never fully live out all the values that I aspire to at the same time, and, in fact, sometimes those values actually compete and then I have to make hard and tragic choices. But being thrown into the world, I don't have any option other than making such choices.

Sometimes I'll present an ethical dilemma in class, something really tough (unlike the easy ones I've been giving you) and I'll ask the students to vote on the right thing to do, and there are always some who won't vote. I will say, "Tell me what's going on here." They say, "Well, there's good arguments to be made on both sides and I feel very strongly both ways." I say, "I understand that, but let's talk about life now. You are going to have some forced choices in your life and you're not going to be able to stand back and say, you know, those were really good arguments on both sides. Eventually you're going to have to act, and there's a certain kind of tragedy to that."

Let me go back to the grim story I told earlier about the woman and her son. There's a lot at stake. I really just want to talk about the ethics part but I also have to talk about the personal part. Here she is feeling enormously guilty for a choice she made to end her son's life a few days or weeks before it would have ended if she had allowed a different course of action, and now she wants to know if what she did was right or wrong.

The first thing I say is this: "How can my opinion possibly matter about this? If I tell you that what you did was right will you let yourself off the hook?" And the answer of course is no. "If I tell you that you did something wrong are you going to take that as gospel and beat yourself up more?" The answer to that is probably yes. The plain fact of the matter is my opinion doesn't matter at all.

"Now let's talk about something else," I say. "I want you to suppose that the action that you took was the wrong action. That you acted unethically. Let me talk to you not as an ethicist but as a theologian. I think the minute you did that God forgave you. And the real question here is, are you going to be able to forgive yourself or not? And if that was a bad choice, it will not be the last one you make in your life, and we really have to believe that salvation happens through faith in God's grace, not because we're such great ethicists. Now that's it. In the moment did you do the best you could?"

And she says, "I don't know." That's a good answer. When I ask my students who do badly on a test if they studied, they usually say something like, "I did the best I could." And I say, "Really! You couldn't have studied five more minutes?" "Oh yeah, I guess so." "Well then, you didn't do the best you could?" In fact, the "best you could" is a meaningless concept. In the moment did you do what you thought was right? Yeah. Did you do it before God? Yeah. That's as close as I can come to the best we can do. "Let me help you understand why there's such tension about this. There are two values in your life that you feel very strongly about. One of those values is the sanctity of life. Life is a gift from God and human beings do not have the right to do whatever they want with that life. That life has the value, not that I place on it, but that Almighty God places on it. And just because I don't like the cards I've been dealt in my life doesn't mean I can just do anything I want with my life. That's a value I hold to deeply, especially among spoiled Americans who think they have a right to life on their terms. But the other value that you hold very deeply is relieving suffering, doing good, preventing harm, caring for and protecting the people you love. That's another value I hold deeply, as you do. You found yourself in that tragic position where to say yes to one meant not being able to say yes to the other, and that's when we have a genuine ethical dilemma. And that's why ethics is ultimately tragic."

I don't think the way to solve such dilemmas is to immediately kick into cost benefit analysis. I don't know if you can tell—I'm not a utilitarian. I think that if you make all decisions on cost benefit analysis, you're going to do some really bad things in your life. What we do in those cases is try to weigh those conflicting duties and decide which one we think carries greater weight. And here's the tragic part again—there is just no formula for doing that. Sometimes one value carries greater weight, sometimes another one.

Whenever I get to this point, somebody says, "Now you're doing situation ethics." Let me pause for a moment. There is a word for ethicists who do not take the situation seriously. It's "stupid." The context, the situation, is very important in our decision making. I'll trot out Rahab as an example. In her particular situation, the value is placed on protecting the spies in God's mission and this purpose trumps truth-telling, even though in the vast majority of cases in Scripture, truth-telling would trump almost everything else.

So how do I figure out how to do that? I don't know. I do have a system that I use, but I've found it doesn't really work. I think what we do is try to recognize the values that are in conflict with another, and that helps us think through the problem. We take those values very seriously at every moment and then we try to sleep as best we can that night. One of the problems I have with my students is for about ten weeks I'll hit them with dilemma after dilemma after dilemma and they'll come away thinking that the whole world is gray. So note well: the kind of ethical dilemmas I'm talking about here make up about 5 percent of the moral life. The other 95 percent is crystal clear, if you take these values seriously; in these cases the question is not, "What's the right thing to do?" but rather, "Am I going to do what I fully know is the right thing?"

Chapter Five

THE SUBVERSIVE ETHIC OF CRUCIFORMITY

Now I want to take the next step, because when you bring Jesus into the equation things start to get tilted somewhat. Jesus is going to push us towards not just being minimally decent Samaritans, but Good Samaritans. So I want to think about how ethics gets radicalized by Jesus' view of the world.

I am not just a philosophical ethicist; I'm also a Christian theologian who claims to be a follower of Jesus. So I want to address Jesus and the ethic we find in his teachings. There was a recent book by Brett McCracken called *Hipster Christianity: When Church and Cool Collide*. McCracken observes how many churches, in their desperate attempt to become relevant, have tried to be cool. That's a pretty tough way to go because I don't know if you've noticed but cool is a moving target. The very nature of cool suggests that not everybody can be cool, and if everybody starts to be cool, then cool has to move so fewer people are cool. So if you're chasing cool, you're always going to be chasing a moving target. My spin on this is that at the heart of coolness is subversion. What coolness wants to do is subvert or undermine current norms. And in that sense, Jesus and Christianity are inherently cool because Jesus is deeply subversive. But he is subversive, not for the sake of subversion, but for the sake of the kingdom of God. He brings to us deeply subversive values.

Cross-Shaped Subversion

One of those is the concept of cruciformity, which is a great word we need to be reintroduced to. Cruciformity is a rich word which means cross-shaped. I occasionally tell my theology students, after I've dragged them through lots of really difficult stuff, that to me as a follower of Jesus there is one crucial question, "What are the implications of following a crucified Messiah?" The cross was Jesus' deeply subversive event. He is a crucified Messiah. Of all the ways that God could express himself, he decides to express himself in an act of self-giving, sacrificial powerlessness. So if I'm going to follow this Messiah then my life must become cruciformed. It has to be cross-shaped. Every area of my life. And the implications of following that kind of Jesus are worked out, not just in Jesus' life, but through the rest of the New Testament, and it leads us to a radical expression of ethics that is far beyond what any philosophical system of ethics could provide.

Let me give you a few instances. Ephesians 5:22. Here's where we have a basic lesson in Bible interpretation. The section goes from 5:21 down thru 6:9. The heading for the section is this: submit to one another out of reverence for Christ. That's the point. And then Paul gives us three examples of what that means. He gives the example of husbands and wives, the example of parents and children, the example of slave and master. But if you cut off the heading then you don't see what these examples are examples of, which is submitting to one another out of reverence for Christ. And then he gives instructions to those who are both in the power up and power down position, which is a little bit unusual. You would expect to have instructions for the person in the power down position, but giving instructions to the ones in the power up position is a little bit unusual in the ancient world.

For instance, it won't surprise you that I treat the president of my university, my boss, with great respect. That's easy. The question is, "How do I treat my students over whom I have enormous power?" This passage says "submit to one another out of reverence for Christ." And so the question is not just, "How do I lay down my life for those who have power over me?" Rather, the question is, "How do I lay my life down for those over whom I have power?"

Let me see if I can get a bit more practical. If you are a church leader, you probably spend a lot of time in meetings. I'm an academic. My life is one long meeting interrupted by a class from time to time. For church leaders the question is how do I have cruciform meetings? That question would radically change most churches. That is, when I go to a meeting the question is, "How am I going to submit to you out of reverence for Christ? How will I not be manipulative, not get my own way, not be demanding and overbearing, but figure out what it is that God wants to do with you in this situation and submit to that? "

Or if you're a younger person, I think a big issue for you is, "What does it mean to practice cruciform sex?" You see, the real problem with pornography is it's not cruciform. When I use pornography it's all about me; that person or image that I'm looking at is just an object to be used for me and my pleasure. Cruciform sex says that the act of sex is not just about me, it's about me submitting to and caring about and sacrificing for you. If we are going to make any headway on the sexual mess that our world is in, it's going to begin with understanding what it means to live in a cruciform way. It's not about me, my power, my wants, my desires; it's about laying my life down. Now that is a radical revision of the world.

The Stories We Live By

I'm indebted to James Bryan Smith's book *The Good and Beautiful God* for some of the thoughts that follow. Think about the stories or narratives that we live by. That is, at any particular time what story is operative in your life? I used to tell my ministry students that the single most important question to ask yourself as you're dealing with the elders in your church is, "How many of them are products of the Great Depression?" Because for people who lived through the Great Depression that impacts their thinking as much as anything else. Generally people who lived through the Great Depression (like my father) tend to be fiscally cautious. They know what it means to lose everything. They're afraid of debt. But my whipper-snapper students have lived a completely different experience. They think debt is how you live. They're a little confused by money. They understand a credit card. And because they have a different life experience, they interpret as faithlessness what is a different way of seeing the world.

There are certain stories that become a part of us. I have for years taught the capstone course on integration of psychology and theology in our marriage and family therapy program. It's kind of funny when you think about it. I have the shortest premarital counseling sessions of anybody. I just say, "Stick together." And one thing I've learned from counseling those planning to marry is that if people learn fundamental mistrust early in their life through child sexual abuse that becomes part of their story, it is a very difficult story to rewrite. It's not impossible. It's just really hard. And so we all have these different stories that are operative.

One of my favorite studies in the field of behavioral economics involves a situation where the researchers create a test for students where they're encouraged to cheat. Then with a control group and another group they analyze how much cheating has been done. They have one group write down their ten favorite movies and they have the other group write down as many of the Ten Commandments as they can remember. Now what's fascinating about this is the group that has to write the Ten Commandments cheats less than the other group. It doesn't matter how many of the Ten Commandments they can remember. It doesn't matter if they can just remember two, three, or five. The overall cheating goes down, which is really interesting because the Ten Commandments are somewhere back there in their story and when that story is brought to the fore, they are more likely to act out of it.

Fear and Power

James Smith holds the opinion (as I do) that the primary story out of
which we work is fear and power, which are closely related. Most of what
we do is out of fear and power as the way to control the fear. The reason
we're so tribal is we are threatened by another group, but if I have more
power than that group then I don't have to be fearful of it. Smith tells
a story about a bunch of preachers who are at a big event and Dallas
Willard is speaking. Willard says, "I'm going tell you the single most
important spiritual discipline in your life." It gets deathly quiet and everybody is leaning in because Dallas Willard is God's best friend. He says,
"Here's the most important discipline for your life: pray for the churches
around you." He says that because he believes that the vast majority of
preachers and pastors are driven by fear; they see the churches around
them essentially as competitors.

The story of fear and power must be replaced by another story. Smith
says, "Here's your story: 'you are a member of the kingdom of God and
the kingdom of God is never in trouble,' and if you start to believe that,
then fear and power no longer become the operative story in your life. If
you believe that the kingdom of God is never in trouble, then it frees you
to practice the self-sacrificial, other-regarding love the way Jesus shows
us on the cross."

It's interesting to me that in all the passages that talk about the resurrection of Jesus, there's never a suggestion that Jesus raises himself. God
always raises Jesus up. Indeed, I hold the view that Jesus does not have
the ability to raise himself, that when Jesus takes the sin of the world on
himself at the cross he essentially experiences hell for us—this is ortho-
dox Christianity—and he then waits for God to rescue him from Hades.
In other words, the cross is Jesus' absolute expression of total trust in
God. I believe that at any point Jesus could have jumped off the cross and
called on angels. Rather than becoming the source of his own security
and working out of fear and power, he says, "I'm will trust God to care
for me." So God raises him up.

Who Has the Power?

That's the story Christians are trying to live into and it leads into a much more radical expression of ethics. I'll hit you with two passages really quick here. One of them is the Sermon on the Mount—a passage that I am convinced I have misinterpreted pretty much my entire professional life. I am grateful to Glenn Stassen, *Living the Sermon on the Mount*, for showing me this. It is easily the single most difficult passage in the Sermon on the Mount. Matthew 7:6, "Do not give dogs what is holy and do not throw your pearls before pigs." We know this is not about dogs and pigs. These dogs and pigs are people. It already bothers us that Jesus is calling people dogs and pigs. If you're reading the NIV, the section break is very interesting here. The NIV is convinced that verse six goes with verses one through five. That Jesus gives some instruction on not judging and then basically comes down in verse six and says, I don't mean don't judge at all. Here is some judging you should do—which is the way I've taught it.

I've now become convinced that the problem is that verse six does not go with verses one thru five. We've got it divided up wrong. Verse six goes with verses seven thru twelve. Listen to how it sounds if you put verse six with what follows: "Do not give dogs what is holy and do not throw your pearls before pigs lest they trample them underfoot and turn to attack you. Ask and it will be given to you. Seek and you will find. Knock and it will be opened to you, for everyone who asks receives. The one who seeks finds and the one who knocks it will be opened or which of you if his son asks for bread will give him a stone or if he asks for a fish will give him a serpent. If you then who are evil know how to give good gifts to your children, how much more will your father who is in heaven give good things to those who ask him. So whatever you wish that others would do to you do also to them, for this is the law and the prophets."

So think this through with me for a minute. See if I can convince you as I've become convinced. If you're a Jew, what kind of people would be dogs and pigs? Gentiles. Now if we're not just talking about pigs but we're talking about dogs, what particular kind of Gentile? Romans. Occupying

Roman soldiers. It's in the literature. Dogs. Pigs. So what if he's saying this? Don't give what is sacred—your trust, your commitment, your security—to dogs and pigs, that is, to the Roman Empire. Instead find your security, not in the government, but in God because he'll give you everything you need. Because even though you being evil know how to give good gifts, how much more will your Father in heaven give to those who ask him. And so what the passage is essentially doing is subverting any effort to trust in worldly Roman power for one's security; instead, one trusts God who gives generously. One of the reasons why we struggle so much with generosity is because we do not believe in the good provision of God. Once you come to believe in the generosity and the provision of God it becomes much easier to be generous with other.

Trusting in Lamb Power

Let me come to my favorite book of the Bible—Revelation. Chapter five is one of the more important turning points in the Book of Revelation. I need to get a running start towards it so I'll start with verse one, but what I'm really interested in is the transition between five and six. "Then I saw on the right hand of him whose seated on the throne a scroll written within and on the back sealed with seven seals and I saw a strong angel proclaiming with a loud voice who is worthy to open the scroll and break its seals and no one in heaven or on earth or under the earth was able to open the scroll and look into it and I began to weep loudly because no one was found worthy to open the scroll or look into it. And one of the elders said to me, 'Weep no more; behold the lion of the tribe of Judah of the root of David has conquered so that he could open the scroll and its seven seals. And between the throne and the four living creatures among the elders I saw a lamb standing as though it had been slain with seven horns and with seven eyes which are the seven spirits of God sent out into all the earth."

Did you see that? Who can open the scroll? The lion of the tribe of Judah. And then who opens the scroll? The lamb who had been slain. The author intentionally flips from lion to lamb and then through the book of Revelation it is lamb to the end. The book of Revelation is about lamb power. The author takes on the image of lion, which is one that would be associated with Rome, and then intentionally subverts the image, saying the conquering is going to be by the lamb. The question then is, "Do you believe that or not?" That's what he's asking these Christians. Do you believe in lamb power? Because when you look out your window you see all the power of the Roman Empire and you think it's going to exist forever; but what I'm trying to tell you is that the power of the lamb can overcome all that. Do you believe that? If you do you don't give your trust and security to Rome.

If you think I'm just making this up you could come to Revelation 13 where I can tell you what 666 means and who the beast is. He's giving these pictures of these two beasts and then we do back flips trying to figure out what 666 means. It's really not that complicated. When you see his description of the two beasts, anybody in the first century could have immediately identified them. The first beast is the Roman Empire and the second beast is emperor worship; there's nothing mysterious about it at all. The riddle is not who they are but what the right name is for them.

Have you ever noticed that you name your pets too early? You know, you've got find out what they're going to be and then you name them. Same way with children in some cases. If you'd wait a while you're more likely to get the name right. And those of you who read a little Greek know there's this odd thing in Greek: there is no indefinite article. (I know you didn't pick this up for a Greek lesson and you do not have to know Greek to get to heaven—you just won't be able to talk to anybody when you get there.) There is no indefinite article in Greek. There is no "a." The best example of the importance of the indefinite article is this: suppose that you have the world's biggest stage and you're going to say exactly one line and this line is going to go down in history. This is the situation that Neil Armstrong is in before he gets ready to step on the moon. He just has one line and he blows it. He claims he didn't blow it, but I've listened. He blew it. He uttered a line that makes absolutely no sense. He said, "That's one small step for man, one giant leap for mankind." What he meant to say was this: That's one small step for *a* man, one giant leap for mankind. Which would have been brilliant. I feel a little sorry for him. He claims he said "a," and there is now a great internet debate about it.

So there is no indefinite article and so in verse eighteen you have "for it is the number of a man"; " a" is not there. It could be "for it is the number of man" or it could be "it is the number of a man," and there's no way in Greek to know which is the correct translation. I'm absolutely convinced that what it says is "for it is the number of man," because what's the Roman emperor claiming? He's claiming to be God. He's claiming to be divinity and so he says you have these two beasts. You have the Roman Empire. You have emperor worship. And now let's assign the right name to them. The name we're going to assign them is 666, for it is man's number. Do you see what he's saying? After all the pretensions and claims of the Roman Empire, when you peel back the curtain, guess what you see. Just human. All too human. In fact, I call this the Wizard of Oz verse of the Bible. You see the image of the mighty wizard. But roll back the curtain and guess what you see? An insignificant little man! That's what the Roman Empire is made of, and what the author is doing is stamping 666 on every human enterprise, and saying, "When you trust in that stuff, when you trust in power, you're trusting in human stuff. What you should be trusting is lamb power." And if you believe that, it releases you from fear and allows you to engage in cruciform, self-sacrificing, self-giving love because you know God's got you.

I got the same call that many of you did a couple of years ago from my money manager. She calls and says, "I guess you've seen what's happening to your investments?" And I said, "Yeah, as a matter of fact I did." And she said, "I just wanted to make sure you weren't getting ready to jump off a bridge." I said, "We live in Abilene, Texas. Bad choice. I might could shoot myself. Guns are cheap and plentiful here." And I added, "You know, we just don't know each other well enough. I have not thought about suicide a single time. I've been thinking about homicide almost continually and you really ought to stay on your side of town until you have a little differ-ent news to deliver." I knew she wouldn't get it, but I couldn't resist. I said,

"There's some stuff I'm worried about, but this is not one of them because these accounts have a number and their number is 666. It's human stuff. It's passing away and if all the financial structures in the world fall away, there's still lamb power." And that is amazingly freeing.

A More Radical Ethic

I don't know if you've noticed, but all those ethical theories I was discussing early on deal with how we can live with each other without killing one another. How can we have a world where we don't have to live in constant fear of one another? It's all about balancing power and rights and all of those things. Then Jesus comes along and says, "Let me give you a far more radical way. Let me give you cruciformity, where you can lay down your life because you know that God will lift it up." Where your concern is always for the other as an act of mutual submission, because you know that God's got you. And when you find your security in God all of those things we do out of fear and power to protect ourselves start to fall away.

You know, one of the things that's frustrating to me is that there are some areas of my life that look pretty cruciform and there are other areas that cruciformity has hardly touched. I want to know what it's like to live out of that kind of trust and have my life ordered that way. I want to know what it's like not to be constantly living out of fear and constantly trying to balance power.

This perspective takes us into a much more radical place. It takes us to a place where only a follower of Jesus, in my opinion, can adopt that stance; and there's something wrong with asking people who haven't made a commitment to Jesus to do that. People who haven't made a commitment to Jesus I'm going to ask to be minimally decent Samaritans. Live out of those principles. But to those who have confessed Jesus as Lord, I want to ask something more; I want to call you to cruciformity and ask, "What happens when we start to live out of the cruciformed life?"

Chapter Six

FIVE PRINCIPLES OF THE CRUCIFORMED LIFE

I argued in the last chapter that we have these competing stories by which we attempt to live. Scripture offers us the cruciformed story. Therefore, the cross is not just the means of our salvation; the cross is the story that we are to live out. We have a really hard time doing that because the world pushes upon us the story of fear and power and that story often overwhelms the self-sacrificing story of the cross.

My task in this chapter is more difficult. I want to say something about what that life looks like in as practical a way as I can. I will set forth five principles of the cruciformed life. I want to say at the beginning that's the best I can do. I'm in no position to tell you at any particular instance what the cruciformed thing to do is. I have to leave that to your good conscience and your knowledge of Scripture, Jesus, and the situation.

Candor About Our Fears

Principle number one. Since the story of fear and power is constantly working around us and in us, one should always put that on the table rather than having it under the table. This is doing nothing more than admitting our fallenness and the way we often fall into the story of fear and power. It is an act of self-reflection and disclosure that is absolutely crucial.

So I'm having a conversation with somebody. We're trying to figure out what to do. Somewhere in that process I probably need to say something like this, "Here's the anxiety I'm feeling. This is what I'm afraid of. This is what I think ought to happen and I am feeling a great need to create this solution." Do you hear what happens there? All those things are operating whether I admit it or not. If I face it and put it on the table, then we can all look at it, and it is much less pernicious and dangerous on the table than it is under the table. In other words, we need to replace passive aggressive with aggressive aggressive. That way we always know where we stand.

I think one of the healthiest things that church leaders could ever do is in meetings where they're going to make crucial decisions to go around the table and let everyone identify what they are bringing to this problem besides the word of God. What I'm bringing into the room is I'm really afraid about the future of this church and I don't want it to disappear on my watch. What I'm really afraid of is if we do this, then some of my peers will not have as much respect for my work as they currently do. What I'm afraid of is what my parents will say. All those things are operating and once we identify them they're not free to do their sneaky work. They don't get eliminated but at least we can look at them now.

We're afraid. I am afraid to face the fact that I'm not as pure in this as I like to believe. In other words, I'm human. Who wants to admit that? When somebody says to me, "You think you're right about everything," my response is always, "What was your first clue?" Of course, I think I'm right about everything. Every sane person I know thinks they're right about everything. Think about it. Why do you hold the views that you hold? Because you think they're wrong? Nah, you hold the views you hold because you think they're right. Now, your experience has told you that sometimes you've been wrong, but you don't know what you're wrong about now because if you did you would have changed your mind and you would be completely right again. Everybody thinks they're right about everything. Put it on the table. Of course I think I have the best idea on this. Of course I think I have the right theology on this. But those views aren't pure. They're tainted by my fear and my anxiety and my need to control, so I need to be able to look at that and you need to be able to look at that. If we could actually do that, it would be much harder to make non-cruciformed decisions because we have our eye on it now.

I tell church leaders that if you do not have heresy consistently spoken in your church you are not doing it right, because people have wacky ideas. The question is, have you created an atmosphere where they feel free to put them on the table or not? If they don't put them on the table, I promise you they don't go away. They just go under the table, and you don't want them there. You want things where you can talk about them.

And so we should confess our fears and our concerns. I need to be able to say, "I'm afraid for us to do this because I'm afraid we'll be under the judgment of God and we might go to hell if we do this." I want to hear those words. I want to put it on the table so I can look at it and I can deal with it. It works a lot better if I'm able to point that out about myself instead of having you point it out about me, because that's harder to take. We need to get into the exercise of offering it up ourselves, and then asking, "Is there anything else anybody sees going on here with me that I'm not seeing?" Because sometimes I just don't see it.

Practice Obedience

Number two. Practice submission or obedience. I refer to the Hebrews passage that says Jesus learned obedience by the things that he suffered, and that's what makes him our perfect high priest. Now, if you think about it, that's bizarre. Jesus Christ, Son of God, omniscient one, learned obedience. Because obedience is one of those things that you only learn by experience. It cannot be learned theoretically. There are some things that can be learned theoretically. But obedience can only be learned in practice. There is no other way to do it. And so we need to regularly practice submission and obedience.

I really struggle with obedience and I can tell you why. Because I am right about everything (of course! See previous section). And obedience for me almost always means placing myself under someone who is less well informed than me. And I would at least venture the notion that obedience or submission may only be learned in such circumstances. Here's a tough example.

I sometimes spend my vacations in ways not everybody would choose. I like to hang out with monks and hermits and other assorted people who don't want anything from me. Very quiet. A lot of these places tend to be Catholic, because we don't have a lot of Protestant monasteries. At one particular place they speak a very powerful rhetoric of Christian unity. I like that because my Christian tradition also speaks that rhetoric powerfully. But when it comes time to do communion they won't allow me to partake with them because I'm not a Catholic in good standing. So I say to the leader, "You have this rhetoric of Christian unity, and we come to this fundamental symbol of Christian unity and you won't let me do this and your actions speak louder than your words." And he says very gently, "I understand what you're saying. I really do. I'm sympathetic to it. But I must be in submission to the church." Now I'm not sure who's got the right end of this argument. But at that moment I was deeply appreciative of his willingness to be obedient to a position that he thought was wrong.

There's a tension between this call to do what we think is right and the need sometimes to be submissive or obedient to others. I'm not here today to sort that out in every case. I don't have the first idea how to. I do think that we have not taken seriously enough the notion that we learn submission and obedience to God by practicing submission and obedience to one another. And there surely must be some circumstances in which I do not have to have my way. Surely there are some times when the principal of submission trumps being right. Or as my friend Paul would put it, "Knowledge puffs up, but love builds up."

I think there are times when one must be disobedient and I don't have any rules for exactly when that is. I think, again, it requires great maturity to know those times when the rules absolutely must be broken for the sake of the kingdom of God. But as I examine my own life, I know that I am better at breaking the rules for a good cause than submission and obedience, which means I need help in leaning into submission and obedience. Jesus Christ learned obedience by the things that he suffered, and so the call here is for the obedience to the way of the cross to be one of the primary markers of our life. Now that's scary because if you are as brilliant and well informed as I am, it means having to submit to those who aren't (of course!). And that always seems like a bad idea. Always. But I must lay that aside and say I need to be obedient.

Choose the Side of the Weak

Number three: move towards weakness. There are going to be times in our lives when we have to pick a side. Now it's one of the principles of my life not to pick a side if I don't have to. And I don't consider that a sign of weakness. I consider that a sign again of my deep maturity (of course!). There are times when you've got to pick a side and I think that if you're going to err, you should err on picking toward the side of weakness, picking toward the side of the oppressed, picking toward the side of the losers, picking toward the side of those who cannot take care of themselves. If there is a biblical doctrine of the use of power, I would venture that it is if you're going to use power you're always going to use it in behalf of those who don't have much. You don't use power to prop up your own position. You don't use power on behalf of yourself. You use power in behalf of the other. I want to do my best to make sure I don't find myself fighting against God, and he's got a way of lining up with the powerless and the losers and the throwaway people. If I'm going to err, I want to err in that direction. I want to err in joining the side of the weak.

Let me tell you a story about a former student. He's one of the most brilliant students I've ever taught. He wasn't glib brilliant, he was deep brilliant. He was the kind where you would deliver a lecture and he wouldn't say a word. He would go home, think about it overnight, come back the next day, and take you apart. He'd see every problem.

He'd see the right questions to ask. Just an extraordinary mind. And at one point he's getting ready to graduate and I said, "What are you going to do when you graduate?" And he said, "I am going to go pick tomatoes in the Dominican Republic." And I said, "Explain this to me." He says, "I want to live in solidarity with the poor. I think that's what I'm going to do." And I said, "Don't do that. You've got a once in a decade mind among the students I've taught. If you really care about the poor go to Harvard Law School, get yourself some power, and rock the world." He paused as he almost always did and he said, "That might not be a bad plan except for one thing." I said, "What's that?" He said, "I know myself well enough to know that if I do that I will become what I despise." And I thought, go pick tomatoes. Boy, that's a rare kind of personal insight, isn't it? Here's somebody who understands that using power even for good causes has its own kind of corrupting influence.

There are a lot of different ways of lining up with the poor and the oppressed and the powerless. You have to leave it to your own judgment about your character and the way God has wired you and which ways you can do that and which ways you can't. But I think when we come to pick a side, we better make sure that we tend to pick the weak and powerless. The powerful don't need you, and God just doesn't line up with those who have all the power.

Engage with Open Hands

Number four. This is by far the most important. Forsaking power for cruciformity does not mean passivity. What it means is when you engage, you engage with open palms, not clenched fists. What it means is you are going to trust God to be able to do the heavy lifting and that you do not have to control the situation. You don't have to manipulate the situation. You do not have to use the sinister works of power. If you're available to God and will unclench your fists, God will use you in cruciformed ways. You remember that song we used to sing—with that great line about Jesus on the cross? "He could have called ten thousand angels." All the power of heaven dwarfs anything that human beings have. Engaging the world with the power of God rather than human power only makes sense.

Now, in practical terms what does this mean? It means we are going to practice extraordinary times of silence. Silence is the discipline that teaches us almost everything. As I'm talking, I am manipulating the way you perceive me. I'm presenting myself in a certain way. When I go silent I no longer have the ability to do that and I have to stand before God as who I am. When I am silent in situations where I would normally speak, I release my power to control the situation and place it instead in the hands of God.

I feel as if I talk way too much. I get paid to talk. I get paid to go to church. I don't know if I'd go for free or not! I'll have to think that one through a little bit. And when you get paid to talk, you tend to do it all the time. So I got to this point where I needed to be much quieter. I was in this big, important meeting and I had made this deal with myself that no matter what happened in this meeting I was going to say nothing. I was going to practice the discipline of being quiet. For a while I carried around this rock in my hand as a constant reminder that I had nothing meaningful to say. Listen to the rock. So I'm sitting there and at points gripping my rock, you know, because it's clear that this group needs my guidance (of course!). I managed to get through the whole couple of days of meetings without saying a word. Then somebody at the meeting said, "Look, everybody is wondering if you're for or against this stuff. You've been so silent. Everybody is wondering what you're thinking." And I thought, what a mess I have made of my life. I have talked so much that people assume when I'm quiet something must be wrong. How am I ever going to fix this? And so my solution was to just start talking again.

That act of silence is one of the more powerful ways to open your palms. Another way of opening your palms is to give up our fetish of outcomes, because outcomes depend on a wide variety of things. This has been one of the harder lessons to learn as I work with my congregation of eighteen to twenty-two-year olds. I consider myself a minister just like many of you do. It just happens that my ministry is with a group of young people who rotate through. (I'm sure some of you would like to have a church like that.) And eighteen to twenty-two-year-olds will occasionally make less than optimum decisions. And I have this deep need to control, to fix, to guard, to make sure—and that will keep you awake at night. But I've gradually learned to release my grip and say what I'm going to do is this: "I know God is working in this kid's life and I'm going to join God in what he's doing and then I'm going to let it go." I tell parents who occasionally call me about their children, "Look, you never had much control. You lost most of it when they went to kindergarten and you don't have any now. Release your grip. Release them unto God. Try to join God in what he's doing." This is not passivity; this is engagement, but its engagement with open palms, not clinched fists.

I'm thinking about my friend Dietrich Bonheoffer. (Have you noticed how many of my friends are dead? You can have friends who are dead! In fact let me bear witness. It is easier. In order of preference there are my dead friends, my virtual friends, and then the flesh and blood ones.) Dietrich Bonheoffer says that ministers must never become the accusers of their churches. Instead of accusing their churches before God, they lift them up and they hold them up before God. You have very little control over your church. And to be able to engage that group of people and try to lead them in cruciformed living and then at the end of the day be able to open your palms and leave them in the good hands of God is in many ways the key to cruciformed ministry. As long as we think we have to keep a stranglehold on things, it's going to be hard to be cruciformed. Cruciformity is an act of letting go and trusting God.

I have a fairly driven personality. I admit it. I don't know how that happened. My brother is not like that. I think my brother will be dead a week before anybody notices. He's very calm and I am driven and, boy, this has been such a hard lesson. I'll bring Eugene Peterson to my side. Peterson points us to the rhythm of nature where he says the rhythm of early Genesis is evening- morning, day one. Evening-morning, day two. And in the rhythm of nature before technology, you work all day and then you go to bed at night because it gets dark. The theory is that you are in charge of things during the day, but then when you go to bed at night God comes on duty. Isn't that beautiful? That means every time you take a nap the world is in better hands. Now I'm willing to bet there is not one minster reading this who believes that, who really lives into the reality that it's in God's good hands. It's not that I don't want to be engaged, it's just that I'm going to unclench my fists, quit trying to have my own way, quit trying to control the world, quit trying to do with power what can only be done with trust.

Love Relentlessly

Point five: relentless love. I'm always uncomfortable talking about love, because it sounds so Pollyannaish. I raise questions about why people keep having children, knowing that children are likely to be the single greatest source of pain in life. There are people all over who know how not funny that is. You had such hopes for who your children were going to be as children of God and it didn't turn out that way. And that has caused you greater pain than any single thing in your life. When you have children that's always a possibility. Now maybe some people aren't thinking about it as much as they could. It's like a cute puppy. You see that cute puppy and you forget that he's going to ruin your life for the next fifteen years. I'm sure there are some people who are seduced by the baby.

But at a deeper level, people keep having children because they believe love is worth the risk. Which is the same reason that I believe God created the heavens and the earth. He knew what risks were involved in creating creatures like us. He just thought love was worth it. Everything in the universe is reaching towards the love of God and at the end that love will be all in all. The only thing that makes sense in this life is to act towards all creation the way God does, with relentless love. Love and power are deeply antithetical to one another. For love to be love it must be free, and that's hard. Sometimes I think we would rather control than love.

As an educator at a Christian university, I struggle with the fact that I cannot teach my students to think and then control how it's going to come out. If I empower them to think, and empower them to make their own decisions, I can't determine how that's going to come out. It often doesn't come out the way I wanted it to.

It's the same risk God took. He said I'm going to create human beings who have the ability to think and to decide, because I think love is worth the risk. The act of cruciformity is the act of giving relentless love to all of God's creation. Now we could ask lots of hard questions if this was an ethics class, because it's not always clear to me exactly what the loving thing is. But in the biblical witness to Jesus I get a reasonably good shot at figuring out how love works. So to become a follower of Jesus is to enter into the school of relentless love to see what love looks like in various situations and to learn how to love.

It's one thing for me to love you. It's another thing for me to love you *well*. How do I love others in ways that lead them deeper into the heart of God and the following of Jesus? I have to keep asking myself as I'm dealing with my students, "How do I love them well?" If I let them get away with x y z, am I loving them well? If I throw the book at them for an infraction, do I love them well? I have to keep asking this question. How do I love you well? How do I love you in ways that allow transformation to take place?

Now that's as close to practical as a philosophical theologian can get. I know I didn't answer all of your questions, but you shouldn't be asking them. So here are the principles. Put our fears and our anxieties and our power on the table so we can look at it. Practice obedience and submission. Move towards weakness. While you engage, unclench your fists and open your palms, and always lean into relentless love.

Now that's not exactly a recipe. Have you ever noticed that people who write recipe books only write them for people who already know how to cook really well? I'm looking at a recipe book and it's got instructions like "fold in whipped cream." And I had a terrible time trying to fold it! It didn't make sense. At one point I bought a book called *The Absolute Goof Proof Microwave Cookbook*. Do I have a scoop for her! The book is misnamed. It is possible to goof up the recipes in that book. I have offered you no clear recipe for cruciformity. I do not believe such a thing exists. Once we understand the trajectory and the aspects of cruciformity, then what you have to do is work it out on a case by case basis. There's no way I could address all of those cases and, if I did, I'm sure I wouldn't get them all right. (Although I would think I did!) This is the best I can do. This is what it looks like.

Cruciformed Churches

Next I want to engage the question of what a cruciformed church might look like, and apply this to a community of people. One of the questions that I get asked a lot is how to measure how your church is doing or, more often, how our minster is doing. And that is actually an incredibly difficult question to answer. We don't have a lot of good measurements to tell us how we're doing. Not to mention that significant thinkers like Jesus complicate this. The kingdom of God is like a mustard seed, you know. So how are we doing? Well, it's a little hard to know. It's like seeds sown on a certain kind of ground and it appears to be doing really well and then it doesn't do so well; so this business of trying to evaluate how we're doing is actually more complicated than you would think.

I live in an environment—the academic environment—which today is all about assessment. Some of us teach like the good old days—when we just told you what we were doing and you believed it. But now it's not enough for me to say what I'm teaching. People actually want to find out if the students are learning what I'm teaching. Which really slows down the work. So we spend an inordinate amount of time trying to figure out if we really are getting done what we say we're doing. We have assessment agencies that come in to try to help us do that. It's always interesting in the College of the Bible where one of our goals is the spiritual formation of our students. What is going to be your means of assessment? My suggestion is that we hire private detectives to follow our students around for a year, and we will find out how we're doing. Do you see our problem? I might ask a student, "Are you praying more?" And they might be, but if in the midst of their praying they are becoming a bigger jerk than they were, that's not exactly the progress I intend.

Well, we have this same complication when it comes to thinking about churches or the kingdom of God. To try to figure out how we're doing, what do we count? Traditionally what are the two things that we accounted? Money and attendance. Or as sometimes ungraciously put, butts and bucks. The problem with that is we are evaluating our churches in the same way that any corporation would. I think we want to evaluate. I think we want to count. But we have to pay attention to what we're counting. So I want to discuss a certain disposition, and then I want to address what I think we should actually be counting to find out how we're doing

Regarding disposition, insofar as churches are cruciformed, they are willing to die. Because that's the mark of cruciformity. The willingness to go to the cross. There's a little church I go to every other year out in the middle of nowhere in a state that's similarly located. It's a wonderful church out in the middle of nowhere. And there are all these other little churches around it. I saw one that had a new building and I said, "They look as if they're doing pretty good." The preacher at the church I was visiting says, "Not exactly. You know, they got down to about fifteen people and then their building burned. So they collected the insurance and built a bigger one, and now they have about eight members." And I'm thinking, talk about being offered deliverance from God and turning it down. I mean, you know, he's offering you this kind of rescue and you refuse to take it. Which is to say it is extremely hard to shut a church. It feels like defeat. It feels like failure.

Or if we looked at it right it could look like the cross. Now churches die in different ways. I'm not necessarily recommending ecclesiatical suicide. Some churches do that. It's like the Kentucky farmer who won millions of dollars in the lotto. Someone asked, "What are you going to do with all this money?" He answers, "Oh, I'm just going to keep farming until it's gone." You know, some churches do that. We're just going to keep doing what we're doing until they're all gone. That's not the kind of dying

I'm talking about. I'm talking about the kind of dying where a church says that we are not the end that we serve. The mission of God and the kingdom of God is the end that we serve. If we give our lives for the sake of the kingdom of God, that looks very cruciformed.

Unafraid Churches

While I was preaching at a church in Nashville, we were getting ready to take some young people down to Guatemala years ago when civil war was going on. Before we left something sort of bad happened there. People wanted to know if we still were going to go. Some asked, "Can you guarantee the safety of our children down there?" "No. I can guarantee you we're not going to be stupid. I can guarantee you we're going to be responsible. But no, I can't guarantee their safety." So some went, some didn't, and the worst thing that happened was some of their luggage didn't get there. So then they come home. A couple of months later they're getting ready to go on their before school trip to Atlanta. We get two of them mugged at gunpoint in Atlanta. And by the way, nobody asked me if Atlanta was safe. They asked me about Guatemala. And of course all these years later I'm still grateful that nobody got hurt and I'm also grateful that they may have learned a very important lesson— that there is no safe place down here.

Here's the biblical principle. If you spend your life trying to make sure that nothing bad happens to you, a lot of really bad stuff can happen to you. You can't live your life in fear. You know, at some point you have to let go of the fear and be bold and live life and throw yourself on the mercy of God. ,

If that's good for individuals, that ought to be good for churches. If what we need to do is to die to become the bloody ground out of which new kingdom work springs, I can't imagine anything more noble for a church that calls Jesus Lord than that. But if we spend all of our time trying to make sure that nothing bad happens to us, a lot of really bad things can happen to us. I would argue the same thing with regard to families. Family cannot be protected. Family can only be extended and if parents spend all of their time trying to make sure that nothing bad happens to their children, a lot of really bad things can happen to their children. What you have to think about is how family gets extended, not how you protect it.

All organizations that wind up being an end in themselves will become self-centered and do bad things. The church has to be an institution that exists for something bigger than itself. It exists for the mission of God. It exists for the kingdom of God. And so we're willing to risk our lives for the sake of the mission that we have been called to. And that's a fundamental attitude shift that has to take place if we're going to have cruciformed churches. You and I may have more invested in a local congregation or a particular denomination than God does. God is invested in the kingdom of God and churches have to be invested in the kingdom of God and religious traditions have to be invested in the kingdom of God. We sacrifice ourselves to that kingdom. That's who we are. That's the fundamental attitude.

The Subversive Church

So what do we count? I'll try this out on you. Let me suggest that what churches should be counting are acts of subversion. Churches are fundamentally subversive groups and we should judge how we're doing by how much subversion we're creating in the world. Now, I'm going to play with the language a little bit because I like to. The reason I prefer the term "subversive" to the term "countercultural" is subversive suggests that I plant myself right in the middle of culture. I'm not going to stand outside of it. I'm going to be in the middle of it and then I am going to live, not by the values of fear and power, but the values of cruciformity. And to do that in the midst of culture is deeply subversive.

What does subversion look like? First-century culture, as best I understand it, was almost totally dominated by class and economic structure. What I would want to do is hang out with people who are of my same class or slightly above so I can climb up. I want you to think about what it sounds like, in a culture like that, for Paul to say, "In Christ there is neither Jew nor Greek, slave nor free, male nor female, they are all one in Christ Jesus." Now that's subversive! I want to know what it was like in the first century for the slave to become an elder before the master did. That must have gotten complicated.

We live in a culture which is not, in my estimation, quite as conditioned by class as that. There's a little more mobility, but exercising true equality when it comes to wealth and poverty is deeply subversive in our culture. We too often have programs to benefit the poor which benefit them at the great expense of their dignity, and I don't think that's exactly what we're after. I don't think we're going to turn people away at the door because of their race, but are we really laying down our own cultural preferences for the sake of the kingdom of God? Like everybody else, I want things my way. I want my style of preaching. I want my style of songs. And the notion that having unity and dignity and equality among races and classes is worth giving up all our preferences is still in our day deeply subversive.

Chapter Seven

THE FULLY MATURE CHRISTIAN IS NOT DISTRACTED

What does it take to be a truly mature Christian? I will not answer that fully, but I do want to introduce some ideas. The first thing I want to say is that reality is your friend. A great deal of maturity has to do with being connected with reality; as we get more mature we should be more connected with reality, not less. But we don't do all that well with reality. What we prefer to do is create a world in our minds that is generally a happier world than the one we actually live in.

What does it mean to live in the real world? It means to live in a world where there is suffering and woundedness and brokenness that you can't fix. The desire to be Mr. or Mrs. Fix It, while well intentioned, is deeply disconnected from reality. I have a psychologist friend who has been reflecting on what it means to grieve with those who grieve. He says that the world is darker than you ever imagined and the pain that can lie in front of you is deeper than you ever thought. To grieve with those who grieve means to crawl into the pit with somebody and be there and know you can't fix it. We have a terribly difficult time doing that. We do one of two things. We try to fix it or we run from it.

We need to face reality regarding the Bible. It is a sign of maturity to start with what's there rather than start with my ideas of what ought to be there. We have a difficult time doing that! I try to be really gentle with my freshman as I lead them into the realities of the Bible, but I do want to lead them into the realities of the Bible. Whatever you think about the relationships between the Gospels, the fact is there are different numbers of blind men in that story and it doesn't help to pretend there aren't. You can explain it in a lot of different ways, but you can't pretend it's not there. You can't pretend those Old Testament stories of genocide aren't there. It's not playing fair to pretend they're not there.

But reality is our friend. We start out with what's real and we go from there. There are interesting studies that come out of cognitive psychology. If you ask a person about a particular aspect of their life, merely asking the question impacts how they think about the rest of their life. For instance, one of the more interesting ones has to do with paraplegics. Someone who has lost use of their legs may be quite happy six months after the loss, if you simply ask them how they are. But if you ask them how they feel about their lives now that they've lost the use of their legs, their reporting on their happiness will be much lower than what you get if you check moment by moment. Are you with me? There is a fundamental disconnect between a moment-by-moment reality and our memory of or reflection on it. (See the monumental work, *Thinking Fast and Slow*, by David Kahneman.)

Now those of us who are somewhat older know this anyway. Memory is highly unreliable. We don't just remember stuff, we create it. We wind up telling a different story than what's really there because somehow we have trouble dealing with reality. I don't know anything good that comes from not being as connected to reality as we can be. Reality is your friend. We have a hard time sharing reality with one another. You could call it lying. I think we would prefer to call it something like finessing.

If I read the Bible correctly and if I look at Jesus correctly, I must conclude that reality is your friend and that one of the deep problems in our lives is we're not living in the real world. That real world is not only darker, more brutal, and painful that we can imagine, it is also more glorious and hopeful and powerful than we imagined. Connecting to that real world is very important to the development of maturity.

The Enemy of Distraction

I want to address what I think is the single greatest impediment to our spiritual maturity. How important do I think this impediment is? You can stack up everything else end to end, put it next to this one, and it will not be half as tall. You can say it in one word: distraction. Distraction is the single greatest threat to our spiritual lives. We are the most distracted group of people in the history of civilization. People have always been distractible, but they haven't always made it a way of life or an art form. A great leap toward Christian maturity is becoming less distracted.

We expect children to be distracted. In fact, we create ways to distract them, but the problem is these days we're never getting over it. We're just distracted from beginning to end. There are serious problems with distraction. First, distracted people cannot pay attention to God in the way that they should. I assume that it is part of our theology that God is on the throne, God's at home, God is speaking, God is communicating, and so whether we are perceiving, seeing, hearing, and understanding God is not going to be so much dependent upon whether God is doing anything as on whether we're paying attention or not. And distracted people cannot attend to God; they cannot properly discern. We have more information and knowledge than any human being can possibly process. The problem is not how much information we have; the problem is being able to discern it, to use it, to make sense of it, to sort it out.

My students are terrible at this. They'll turn in a paper citing something from the internet. I'll go look at it and the few times I can find it (that's my problem, not theirs) I'll take it back to them say, "Who wrote this?" They reply, "I don't know." "How old were they?" "I don't know." They may have cited a seventeen-year-old kid in the paper, but they think because it's on the internet it is good information. Strange.

One of the ways I like to torture my philosophy students is to go in on the first day and say, "I want you to find for me on your iPhone what is the highest mountain in the world." And of course it takes no time at all for them to say, Mt. Everest. So I ask a harder question, "What was the highest mountain in the world before Mt. Everest was discovered?" Finally, one kid looks up and raises his hand and says the highest mountain before Mt. Everest was discovered was Mt. Everest. You don't find the answer to that question by looking on your iPhone; you have to think. This is a simple exhibition that we think that by acquiring more information we can get the answer, when what we really need to do is practice discernment. Distracted people have poor discernment, especially in the spiritual realm.

I occasionally get invited to a church to speak on discernment issues. We'll have an initial meeting with the leaders and in our first hour three different people will step out of the room to answer cell phone calls. And at the end I always say the same thing. This is hopeless, because to really discern you've got to pay attention to each other and you've got to pay attention to God for prolonged periods of time. If you can't do that for an hour, you cannot discern. One reason why we are continually making spiritual decisions that do not correspond to reality is because we are too distracted to discern. This is a genuinely serious problem.

Being Present

Harvard Science Magazine recently did a study that confirms my prejudices. They discovered that the single most important source of unhappiness is the failure to be present to whatever one is doing at the time. That is twice as important as what you're doing. This is counterintuitive. We usually think we're really happy when we're doing something we like and we're unhappy when we're doing something we don't like. But the fact of the matter is what you were doing is relatively unimportant. What was important is whether you were present to what you were doing or not. According to the study, the three times when people would be most present and thus most happy were having sex, playing sports, and having a conversation with a close friend. And some of the other times when people tend to be least happy is when they are on the computer and when they are resting, because when people are not sleeping but resting, they almost never rest because their mind is constantly atwitter with what they're getting ready to do or what's already gone wrong. So the conclusion of the study was that the Christian mystics and the Buddhist mystics have it right. Your happiness is largely dependent on your ability to be present where you are.

I would also argue that the most fundamental Christian discipline is to be non-distracted and present where you are. So if we can learn to connect to reality and if we can learn to be present and non-distracted, then these are the baseline skills that we need to move towards Christian maturity.

I'm not going to get into a wholesale bashing of technology, but I do want to say that forms are never neutral. They're always doing things and so technology is affecting the way we deal with the world and our fundamental sociology, psychology, and spirituality. I'm not going to argue that technology is better or worse; I'm just going to argue that those things aren't neutral. That means we better be very deliberate about the way we enter into that world. We shouldn't be entering into it uncritically, as almost all churches have. They entered into it and never asked a question. They never asked the spiritual questions. What is this going to do to our ability to attend to God? Because distracted people can't pay attention to God and distracted people can't discern. How can we learn to be more present to the people in front of us and to God? The failure to do that is going to keep us from having the spiritual life that we really want.

The Model Human

Now I must argue my case from Jesus. If I can't argue my case from Jesus, it's not worth making. Jesus is one of my favorite people and I take the confession I make about Jesus very seriously. Theology for me is not a parlor game. It is what provides the anchor and the direction of life. I confess that Jesus is fully God and that means when I want to know about God, one of the primary places I look at is at Jesus. The other thing I confess is that Jesus is fully human and that means when I want to know how to do human right, Jesus is the expert. We have always thought about the sinlessness of Jesus as a reflection of his deity. Because he is God, he has the ability to be sinless. But if he is fully God and fully man all of the time, his sinlessness is also a reflection of the way he does humanity. If I have an interest in living a life that is most consistently in sync with the reality of the truth of God, the man Jesus is the one I'm going to look at to see how one might do that.

I'm certainly not going to claim that I can do it as well as he did. What I am going to claim is that he's the model who shows me how. I think that Jesus' sinlessness is a reflection of the fact that he is so attentive to God, that he is so in tune with God. And that is the model for us. What I want to do is to get so in tune with God, be so attentive to God, be so non-distracted and in sync with God, that when I act, I always act out of the Spirit of God within me.

And when we do that life gets much better. Jesus is fully in touch with reality. He's got reality right. He is fully attentive to God. He's so in tune with God that when he acts, he acts out of God with him and that's what leads to the sinlessness of Jesus' life. This grows out of Jesus' prayer life. Jesus is so constantly in touch with God that as he walks through life he thinks God's thoughts after him. I want to offer that this is more possible for you than you think. I want to give you hope that you can experience a spiritual life and maturity that you've hardly imagined.

Let me tell you a quick story, leaving out the names. We have a really troubled student. I was with another faculty member standing outside an office and this student walked out of that office. I know this student vaguely, not well; I saw him come out of the office, he saw me and so I gave him a quick hug and he walked on down the hall. Nothing to it. As he walks down the hall the other faculty member who is standing with me says, "Whoa!" And I reply, "You felt that didn't you." He is so in tune with spiritual realities and has learned to be so attentive that he felt the darkness coming off that young man. This sense is not magic. It's maturity. It is attending to reality and being present. It's being attentive to God over long periods of time so that you start to see the world through God's eyes.

Another example. A minister called me and asked, "When do I totally attend to my particular ministry and when do I speak into our bigger situation at church?" I gave him the advice I give myself. I told him I can solve this problem for you in three words. Trust your prayer. If you pray a lot, you'll be so attentive to God that you think God's thoughts after him, and whenever you're in one of those situations, you trust the Holy Spirit in you to tell you when to speak and when to shut up. It's that simple. There is nothing to it. And it's not magic. He said he understood every word I said but had no idea what I was talking about. And I think that's right. The plain fact of the matter is we haven't made the sort of commitment to prayer that you have to make to actually experience that as a reality. And so in all of those situations we are constantly strategizing, and because we are so disconnected from reality and so distracted, our strategizing will often lead us astray. But it is possible to be so in tune with God that you can talk in a meaningful way about being guided by God. It's not magic. It's spiritual maturity.

How would you like to have your spiritual sensitivities so honed that, though you wouldn't be perfectly aware of what's going on with people, you wouldn't be nearly as in the dark as you are now? What if I could offer you a life where you would actually know when you should shut up and when you should speak? What if you could be totally connected to reality and be so attentive to God that you could actually discern what God was doing in the world? Then you could actually join God in what he's doing in the world. I'm not talking about Wesleyan perfectionism here. But I do think that we can enter into a far different place than we currently are, a place where maturity is not so much measured by a set of religious behaviors, but rather by how in tune with God we are. In such a place we could act in far more redemptive ways in the world.

Chapter Eight

THE FULLY MATURE CHRISTIAN DOESN'T REACT

I want to recommend a book about the ways we think, *Thinking Fast and Slow* by Daniel Kahneman, a cognitive psychologist who won a Nobel Prize. The thinking fast part is about what Kahneman calls system one. It's the system that we normally use. It is the everyday way we deal with the world—largely intuitive and quick; it's the way our minds work about 95 percent of the time. What he calls system two is when we are thinking slow. That's where we have some reason to think that system one may be letting us down so we need to slow down and become more reflective about what we're doing.

So for instance, if I ask you how much is 13 x 24, your system two has to kick in. You don't have an intuitive answer to that. You've got to actually do the math. The following math problem provides a great illustration. A bat and a ball together cost $1.10. The bat costs $1 more than the ball. How much does the ball cost? Everybody's system one says ten cents. But when your system two kicks in, you realize that's wrong because if one is

$1 and the other is ten cents, that's ninety cents difference. Not a dollar's difference. Your system two has to kick in for you to realize the bat costs $1.05. (For some of you there may even be a system three that's still trying to figure out if what I've said about system two is true.)

Another well-documented study is this: If I ask you if Gandhi was younger or older than 144 when he died, most of you would get that right. What's interesting in the experiment is when you follow up that question with this one: how old was he? The vast majority of people who don't know overestimate Gandhi's age just because they were introduced to a totally irrelevant number. Now that one probably ought to concern you a little because, if I want to manipulate your thinking, I can create an irrelevant anchor number and move you to a higher number than you really wanted to go to. You get the idea.

One other helpful insight of the book is that human beings are very risk averse. This is because we suffer more from a loss than we do from a gain we didn't realize. For instance, when you invest in a stock that stock goes down, the wise thing to do is sell it and buy another stock. People will not do that because when they sell it lower than they bought it, they feel like a loser and so they will forego the gains they could make by selling it and buying something better. They suffer the loss more severely than they do the unrealized gains.

You really don't have to understand stocks to understand that. All you have to do is work with church elders. Because, despite some evidence to the contrary, elders are human beings. And they are hard wired like we all are to be risk averse and so will tend to make decisions that minimize losses rather than ones that might give us significant gains if we were willing to take the risk. So I'm actually suggesting that there is some really practical stuff in this highly theoretical book about how we think—and we'll see if it has anything to do with what I'm talking about in a bit.

The title of this chapter is "The Fully Mature Christian Doesn't React," so I want to make a distinction between passivity and non-reactivity, which are not the same thing. It is not to say that Christians are passive—they never do anything, they never respond; it is to say that they are non-reactive. To use the language we used in the last chapter, they are going to act, but they are going to act out of that deepest place in themselves where the Spirit of God and the kingdom of God reside rather than react to the stuff that's happening around them. So when I talk about non-reactivity you shouldn't be thinking of passivity.

Reacting to Circumstances

In broad categories, we react to two things. First, we react to circumstances. Philippians 4:11 reads, "I'm not saying this because I'm in need, for I have learned to be content whatever the circumstances. I know what it is to be in need and I know what it is to have plenty. I've learned the secret of being content in any and every situation whether well fed or hungry, whether living in plenty or in want. I can do everything through him who gives me strength." You may notice that last verse is not about winning a football game. That verse is about being content, and Paul says I've learned the secret of being content in any and every circumstance. I know what it's like to be in desperate need. I know what it's like to have plenty and (my translation of what he's saying) I am relatively indifferent to both because I can do all things through Christ who gives me strength. He's saying that this Christ who lives in him indwells him so deeply that he just doesn't get jerked around by his circumstances the way he did before.

It is the same thing that allows Paul to say, "For me to live is Christ and to die is gain." Now if you're talking about circumstances, death is quite a circumstance. And Paul says, "I am relatively indifferent to the circumstance of life or death." I would love to have that kind of relative indifference to my circumstances. Most of us are just sitting ducks and if we do not develop non-reactivity to our circumstances, we are going to get really jerked around in life because circumstances change rapidly without our seeing it coming. You're healthy one day and you have this disease the next. You know your finances are pretty good one day and the next day they don't look quite as healthy. You thought your family was in pretty good shape one day and you discover the next day they are not.

We must find a way not to react constantly to our circumstances. I think that pushes us way down the road to maturity. I don't want people to be able to tell when I get to work if I have dropped a wrench on my foot on the way. I don't want to be so vulnerable to my circumstances that my clumsiness ruins the rest of my day. Because if I do I'm a sitting duck.

Reacting to People

The second thing that we tend to react to is people. Now I admit I do better with non-reactivity when I do not see people. Those days when I sleep late or stay in my house I do better being non-reactive. People can jerk me around. I don't listen to talk radio because it makes me react and I don't like it when they do that to me. Now there are some people who intentionally cause us to react but most people are carriers of reactivity whether they mean to be or not. You know we're all kind of Typhoid Mary when it comes to reactivity. Much of the time we react to people with defensiveness. It doesn't take very much to put us on the defensive and my experience is that most people are defensive.

Let's suppose that I have a little problem with a company. I call them knowing what's going to happen. I will have to work through a telephone tree to try to get to the one human being in India who can help me; and the truth of the matter is, before I dial the number I am already defensive. I am assuming that they are going to be rude. I'm assuming they're not going to be helpful. I am assuming I'm going to fight for every step. And then I think about these poor people who are talking to people like me all day—and that I'm one of the nicer ones. I had to do something at my bank due to a death in the family and I was talking to my other family members about it. They were explaining what needed to be done and they asked if it will be a problem. I said it doesn't sound like anything that's going to go well. It's just almost unimaginable to me that it will. And it didn't.

We tend not to give people the benefit of the doubt in our conversations. That is, when we can take something either in a positive way or a negative way, we tend to take it in the negative way. And this defensiveness has a way of begetting defensiveness and pretty soon we're not quite dealing with reality anymore. So again I'm wondering if it would be possible to have a life where we are not constantly reacting to our circumstances and to people around us. If you show me someone who never does that, they would come very close to being what I would describe as a fully mature Christian. Total non-reactivity.

The Present Kingdom

Is it possible to do this? I want to start out with one concept and then I will suggest two practices. There is a spiritual leader whom I have always admired, Thích Nhất Hạnh. In my estimation he is the greatest living Zen master in the world. So I go to a retreat Thích Nhất Hạnh is doing in Mississippi. I want you to imagine hundreds of Buddhists in Mississippi. Thích Nhất Hạnh has talked to Christians so much that he's very good at it. And I don't know why, maybe it was just the different angle I was hearing it from, but when he talked about the kingdom of God I heard it in ways I hadn't heard it before. He said the kingdom of God is everything you have ever needed or wanted or longed for in your life and it is fully present in you right now.

Think about that. It's not out there somewhere. The kingdom of God is everything you have ever needed or wanted and it's present in you right now. So his question is, "What's your hurry?" He asks, "Why are you scrambling to get to the next thing since everything you have ever needed or wanted you have right now?" James Bryan Smith, from his Christian perspective, says it this way: "You are a member of the kingdom of God and the kingdom of God is never in trouble."

Now if you believe that concept, non-reactivity becomes much more possible because reaction is a desire to control, to fix; it's striving, trying to make things happen, and if the kingdom of God is already present in you, you can let much of that straining go because everything you ever needed or desired is already yours. Paul would call this "becoming what you are." Paul first talks about who or what you are and then how you seek to live into that reality.

The best way to think about this is marriage. For a Protestant minister the moment you feel the greatest power is at a wedding because it is the only time you've changed the reality of the situation by merely speaking a word. If you're a Catholic you get to do it every Sunday at the Eucharist. But when I say, "I now pronounce you husband and wife," they weren't and now they are. Now, I don't know about her but I can tell you about him. He is going to spend the rest of his life trying to become what I have declared him to be, because he's clueless. He is a husband and now what he's going to try to do is become a husband—to become what he already is.

And so God's work in Jesus Christ has placed the kingdom of God within you. You are this beloved child of God. And if you take that identity seriously, you can live into non-reactivity because you are not trying to grab hold of something that you don't have, you're just trying to live out what you already are. The kingdom of God is everything you have ever wanted or needed and it's fully in you right now; and it is out of that place that we try to live in non-reactive ways. That is the concept.

Intentional Silent Prayer

Now for two practices to help us live that concept. Practice one. We primarily learn to do this by prayer. In Luke 4–6, we have a picture of Jesus who runs off for prolonged times alone with God in prayer. This is the rhythm of Jesus' life. I think it's the secret to his sinlessness, this experience he has with God. If you will look at those passages carefully, you'll see they are really interesting. In Luke 4, Jesus is engaged in some ministry, he goes off to pray, he comes back, and the people say, "We want you to keep doing what you're doing," and Jesus says, "No, that's not why I was sent." I want you to think about that. He goes off for this prolonged time in prayer and he comes back with utter clarity about his calling.

Because of who I've decided to spend my life with, eighteen to twenty-two-year-olds, and an abominable system that requires them to make decisions about their life's work long before they're ready, we often have vocational discussions. What I say to them every time is this, "The decision about one's life's work for a Christian is always an outgrowth of understanding who you are as a person of God." As you get clearer and clearer about that, you get clearer and clearer about the vocational call. Trying to solve that vocational call without understanding who you are as a person of God is really getting the cart before the horse.

Jesus has a relationship with God going which allows him to make correct decisions about his life's work. We have a lot of people who are tenaciously, seriously going about the business of being Christian, they're going straight to heaven, but the sad fact of the matter is that they're not having any fun because they never found their life's true calling. You find that by attending to and paying attention to God. I know that because that's the way Jesus did it.

In Luke 6 before he makes the most important decision in his ministry, the calling of the Twelve, he spends the night praying to God. Which suggests that we probably make better decisions when we pray. I don't think it's so much that God whispers in our ear the right thing to do. I'm not opposed to that, by the way. I just can't figure out how to get in on it. I think as we become more and more attentive to God, as we become more and more what we are, we just make better decisions. We make spiritual decisions because they grow out of our relationship with God and not just our often halting, confused strategizing. I do not think there is any substitute for this. We have to learn to attend to God. What we really want to do is attend to God in the midst of chaos, but the only way you can do that is first learn to attend to God in the midst of silence, because it's easier to do. Then as you learn to do it in silence, you get better and better at doing it in the middle of the chaos.

Now if we get to a point where we perfectly attend to God at every moment then silent prayer or intentional prayer would become totally irrelevant. But since we're not very good at attending to God, we keep returning to our practice of intentional silent prayer before God, because that's the way we constantly learn to attend to God better in the midst of the chaos. There are absolutely no shortcuts on this. If you want to find your life's work, if you want to make better decisions, if want to quit reacting to people and to circumstances, you are going to have to make commitments to prayer that are far beyond what most of us have made.

Those of you who are church leaders are going to have to clear space for prayer, not just for yourselves but for the staff that you have hired. In other words, you're going to tell them, "You will pray or you will be fired because that's job one." Because we need ministers who are non-reactive, who work out of this deep place where the Holy Spirit and the kingdom of God abide, and who work out of that place consistently. Now if Malcolm Gladwell is to be believed, what we need is about ten thousand hours of this; that's the point at which we start to develop some expertise. Some of you need to get started. You do the math on that one. That about three hours a day for ten years or so. After ten thousand hours there seems to be something magic about how we sort of tip over into expertise. I have no idea whether that applies in the spiritual realm or not. It does seem to me that the people who most exemplify the non-reactive life have spent an extraordinary amount of time in prayer.

Slow Goes It

Practice number two: slow down. I do not know whether it is possible to have engaged God in prayer for so long that your immediate, intuitive reaction will always be the spiritual or right reaction. If you ask me for my biases, I do believe that is possible. I do know that until we get there the best suggestion is that in situations where I'm likely to be reactive what I need to do is slow down and give myself a chance to work out of a deeper place. Breathing three times is a really good idea. Whenever somebody is in my office looking for spiritual direction, I always want to say that to myself, "Before you say a word, breathe three times." Give yourself a chance to slow down. Don't react out of the shallow place in yourself. Go deep. Give yourself a chance to find that place where the Holy Spirit and the kingdom of God reside.

That one little suggestion would have saved me most of the big mistakes I have made in my ministry. If I had just slowed down! My first reaction to criticism is to be defensive. If I breathe three times then I can think, "What is there to learn from this?" Usually what I say next to myself is, "After all God spoke through a jackass. It's possible he's speaking through a freshman." Slow down because the wisdom of God comes from radically unexpected places in unexpected ways for those who know how to attend to it. If I can breathe, if I can slow down, I give a chance for my spiritual system two to catch up because my system one is not always to be trusted in this. Now, again, I do wonder whether it is possible for me to engage in prayer so long and persistently that my system one gets totally reworked where my intuitive responses will come from that deep place.

There are certain things that as a baptized person you're not allowed to do. As a baptized person, there are certain things you cannot say. There are certain things you cannot do and if you say or do those things, we throw a flag. And you know, that's actually the language I've tried to learn to use with myself. How do baptized people behave? How does a person who has died with Christ respond to this? And if I can breathe three times and say, "I am a baptized person in whom the kingdom of God resides," then my chances of acting in a non-reactive way go way up. It's that crucial pause and re-orientation that makes so much difference.

I'll address primarily church leaders. We could probably use some better strategy, but that's not where the crisis is. We could probably use some better managers, but that's not where the crisis is. We could probably use some smarter people, but that's not where the crisis is. What we need more than anything else are deeper people. People who work from a level that we too seldom experience. So much of what we do in churches is driven by fear and reactivity; if we could just quit working out of fear and reactivity and work from the Holy Spirit that is in us, I think it would bring radical transformation on our churches.

Chapter Nine

THE FULLY MATURE CHRISTIAN DIES HAPPY

In this chapter I'm going to hit two or three fairly difficult points but in a way that is understandable and so that you can make decisions about them. I try to get my students to think about the following. Assuming the Hindus are not right, you only get one crack at life. You only get to do it once and the question I want them to ask from the beginning is this, when you're on your death bed can you look at your life and say, "That's what I meant to do. My life was good. It had meaning."

My bias is that tends not to happen so much by accident. It happens because you're intentional about living towards that goal. In 2 Timothy 4, almost with his dying breath, Paul says the following, "I'm already being poured out like a drink offering and the time has come for my departure. I have fought the good fight. I have finished the race and kept the faith. Now there is in store for me a crown of righteousness which the Lord the righteous judge will award to me on that day and not only to me but also to all have longed for his appearing." Can you hear it? Paul is saying that's what I meant to do and I'm ready to go now because I did what I meant to do. I fulfilled my life's plan.

Where Things Wind Up

When you get to a certain age you are more willing to say what you really think than you are at an earlier age. I am now at that age. As people have pointed out, I've never been exactly shy about saying what I think. But I want for a moment to address the question of hermeneutics (or how we interpret the Bible). As we are interpreting Scripture and making decisions about our lives, the primary direction that we look is not backwards but forwards. That is, our primary orientation ought not to be to the early church. Our primary orientation ought to be where God is taking all things. We would call this an eschatological hermeneutic because if this is where things are going to wind up the best way to live my life is to get in line with where we're going anyway. So the crucial question is not what did the early church do, the question is where is God taking us. When I am asked to address a question like women's role in the church, whatever conclusions I draw about that are going to be on the basis of this eschatological hermeneutic. That is, what are things going to look like when God is done? That question is more important than what the early church did.

So how do you die happy? How do you live an intentional life where you say that's what I meant to do? The primary orientation of that life is toward the place where God is taking all things.

Consider the chess analogy. When I was first learning to play chess and was getting beaten all the time, I decided to read a chess book to try to get better. I didn't know anything so I just picked the book that had the best title: *How to Win at Chess*. That seems right to the point. And the first line was "Chess players need to learn to think about the end from the very first move." I still tell young preachers when they go to a new congregation that their primary task the first year in a church is not to lose. Never mind trying to win, you're just trying not to give away the game the first six months.

How to Get Where You Want to Go

So as I think about what a mature Christian life looks like, I want to think about it with reference to the end. I think we are correct in the perception that there is some difference between wisdom and knowledge. Some people have lots of knowledge but they don't appear to have much wisdom; and some people seem to have fairly deep wisdom but they don't have as much knowledge. In most circumstances I think wisdom means being able to understand means-end agreement. The wise see what means gets you to the end that you desire, and the people who know how to do that are the people who are wise in that area. So I can have lots of knowledge but never quite get around to understanding the relationship of means and ends.

Don't you often know where you want to go, but you just can't figure out what the series of steps are that will make you wind up there? Church leaders experience this all the time. I experience this with my students. I know where I want them to come out, what they need to be able to do at the end of a class, but sometimes the means I pick never seem to quite get them there. That is, at the end of the class they still can't do what I want them to be able to do. I experience that all the time.

This is where Aristotle is enormously helpful. When Aristotle is thinking about the relationship of means and end, he uses the powerful Greek word *telos*—our goal, our meaning—for end. He wants to know how we live a life that is going to lead us to our *telos*. Now here comes the important part. If you think about this in terms of means-end agreement, there are two ways this can go wrong. One way is to pick an unworthy or bad *telos*. That is, we can commit our lives to a goal that is unworthy of our life and that is guaranteed to make you die unhappy. The way we usually say it is that almost no one on their death bed says, "Man, I wish I'd worked a few more hours. Man, I wish I had acquired a few more things so that I can leave more behind when I die." Almost nobody says that and so when a person picks an unworthy *telos*, we would usually say that they are a bad person because they've picked an unworthy goal in life.

Now most of you are not in that category. My guess is that your *telos* would be a Christian something. The other way this can go wrong is picking an approach to life—the means—which is almost guaranteed to keep you from achieving your end. We would refer to such a person as either confused or, if we're not so generous, stupid. Now, many people including an incredible number of my students, if you ask about the end will give you the right answer. What they don't see is that they are taking an approach to life that is almost guaranteed not to get them to the end they say they want to reach. At that point what I want to say to them is, "You have two choices here. Either get honest about your *telos* or change your strategy." You know, I have admiration for people who pick a rotten *telos* but then build their life around it. At least that's honest. You know at least that makes sense. You want to wind up with all the stuff in the world? Take an approach to life that is going to get you there. But don't tell me that what you really want to do is be invested in your family and then take an approach to life that says the only thing you care about is how much stuff you get. That's dumb. You know, either change your *telos* and get honest with it or change your approach so it matches.

What Do You Really Want?

I can give you dozens of examples, but first let me recruit Jesus for my side—because on any issue I like Jesus on my side. When I look across enemy lines and I see Jesus, I want to change sides. You know, if you're looking for rules to live by, that's one: locate Jesus and go to that side. If I recall correctly, Jesus says something like the following in the Sermon on the Mount: "Don't store up treasures on earth, where moths and rust kind of do stuff to it, but store up for yourselves treasures in heaven." And he says something like, "You cannot serve two masters. You love one and hate the other. For you cannot serve God and money." And he says something like, "Where your treasure is there your heart will be," which intuitively is backwards. We generally think that where your heart is, there your treasure will be; but Jesus says that where your treasure is, there your heart will be. If you really think that through it gets increasingly disturbing.

Let me tell you about a young man at the congregation where I was preaching at one time. I baptized him. He and his wife had met in a bar. She was doing mission work. She was a Christian, he wasn't. They had a good relationship and got married and she got him to come to church; he and I had built a bit of a relationship and I was able to study with him and baptize him. So you've got this relatively new Christian and their marriage starts to go south a bit, so he comes to me for help. This is perhaps not the best source he could go to, but honestly I'm all he's got. I'm the only Christian he has a connection to and that he trusts, so he comes over and we sit down and I say, "Do you want to save your marriage?" "Yes." "How much do you want to save your marriage?" "It's the most important thing in the world to me."

All right, we have a chance. I say, "Let's talk about your life," and like many young people he was remarkably transparent. It's one of my favorite things about young people—and one of my least. As I'm listening to his life, I learn that he was a terrific athlete, and that he was on a really fast track at work. He was investing a lot in it. And he was investing a lot in playing ball with the guys, and there wasn't a whole lot left over for his marriage. I realized that if I waited for him to arrive at the truth they would be divorced in five years, so I asked, "Do you trust me?" "Yes." "Here is the issue. Either you're a liar or Jesus is a liar because Jesus says where your treasure is that's where your heart is; and you tell me your goal is to save your marriage, but all of your treasure, all of your investment is every place else. You have two choices here. Either become an honest man and say my marriage doesn't mean quite as much as you told me it did, or start to adopt a life that will lead you to what you say your goal is."

I cannot tell you how much difference I think that little insight from Aristotle and his friend Jesus would make in individuals' lives and in churches. If churches would be honest about what their *telos* is and then seek wisdom to find the means to achieve those ends, and if Christians would be honest about what their *telos* is and then think about the means that lead to those ends, I think we would get incredibly more healthy. The mature Christian is the one who does that. You start out by thinking about the end.

Here's a passage that we've tended to use as threat rather than promise, Galatians 6 beginning with verse 7: "Do not be deceived. God cannot be mocked. A man reaps what he sows. The one who sows to please his sinful nature from that nature will reap destruction." You sow a certain way, that is the *telos* you wind up with. Then we don't read the next part. "The one who sows to please the Spirit from the Spirit will reap eternal life. Let us not become weary in doing good, for at the proper time we will reap a harvest if we do not give up. Therefore as we have opportunity, let us do good to all people, especially to those who belong to the family of believers."

So he says that if you sow in a certain way it feeds into this *telos* of eternal life, and that investments made there, as Jesus says, are not corrupted by things like rust and moths but are eternally secure. Paul and Jesus are trying to get us to adopt these means if we say we really care about these ends. The person who does that is the one who on the death bed can say, "That's what I meant to do. That's how I intended to live my life."

Outside Our Control

I don't know if you've noticed, but there are significant things in your life and in your world over which you have no control. This has to do with getting reality right. Giving up the illusion that you control the world is absolutely critical because there is much beyond our control. So many people invest so much in trying to protect their family, yet that is something largely beyond their control. Family cannot be protected. The only thing you can do with family is extend it. How do I give family to people who don't have much?

I talk often to parents whose children are making bad decisions. This is what I say to them: "You never had as much control as you thought you did, and what control you thought you had, you lost most of when they went to school and the primary influence in their lives became peers. When they came to college you lost the rest. You have to let it go. You don't have control of this and if you spend your life trying to make sure that nothing bad happens to them, some really bad things can really happen to you and your family."

I was with a couple of former students recently who started adopting children who have special and extraordinary problems, and the life they had planned is not the life they are going to live. The next twenty years of their life has been radically altered. What they can control is the *telos* they choose and even in that situation the *telos* hasn't changed. They intend to continue to be reflections of what the kingdom of God looks like. Because they are baptized people they had already made the commitment that there are no throwaway people in this world, and that regardless of what our society says, everyone is created in the image and likeness of God, and these desperately needy children deserve a life. So they get in the adoption process and they find out that their children have needs that they couldn't even imagine. The thought that we're not going to do this never occurs to them because they're baptized people and they understand that everything they do is reaching toward that *telos*— and they can't control all of the circumstances. They told me they had gotten to a point where they thought they were beyond social embarrassment, but it turns out they had not. So I asked, "How are you and God doing?" And the husband said, "Well, he's hurt my feelings." That's honest. I haven't given up on God. I haven't quit believing in God but he's kind of hurt my feelings. There's so much this man can't control, but what he can control is that he's got the *telos* right. And as life goes on he will keep developing strategies and approaches that are likely to get him to that *telos*. And a bunch of us are going to have to help him.

To summarize, the fully mature Christian deals with reality as it is because reality is our friend. Reality is a reflection of the truth of God. We don't live in our own fantasy world. We don't live in the world of our own making. We live in the world as it really is. The fully mature

Christian attempts to learn to be as undistracted as possible. We're focused and present to God and the people in front of us. In order to live that undistracted life, we spend an inordinate amount of time in prayer, and this prayer is not an attempt to manipulate the world. This prayer is an attempt to see the world through God's eyes, to think his thoughts after him, to love what he loves, and hates what he hates. As we enter into that life, the fully mature Christian gets to the point where theoretically we never react. We don't get jerked around by the people and circumstances around us. Instead, we act out of this deepest place in ourselves where the Holy Spirit and the kingdom of God abides, rather than reacting to what goes on around us. The fully mature Christian leads a meaningful life that leads to a happy death. We do that by being honest about our *telos* and then making a life plan that's likely to lead us there amidst the chaos we cannot control.

My students aren't moved by the concept of heaven as I am. I'm not as moved by it as my parents were. It seems as if the closer your relationship to the Great Depression, the more strongly you feel about heaven. What my students are interested in is how not to waste their lives. They have less concern for streets of gold and more concern for how their lives can count. I've tried to talk about how life counts. It counts by not letting it be a series of accidents, and it counts by making sure that one's life plan matches worthy goals. That's the way to live a meaningful life.

Chapter Ten

GREAT IDEAS FROM OFF-THE-WALL DEAD CHRISTIANS

I want to share some good ideas from off-the-wall Christians. Some of them are just plain strange. Some of them are on the edge of the Christian tradition. Some are very much within the middle of the Christian tradition, but they're just strange people. But I will focus on the ideas that I think are great ideas for our time. They are in every case ideas that permanently changed my life. My four in this chapter are St. Francis of Assisi (my choice for the single weirdest Christian in the history of the world); Soren Kierkegaard, the melancholy Dane, who is truly a weird individual; St. John of the Cross, the great Spanish poet and mystic; and finally St. Benedict, who ran one of his monasteries in such a way that all the monks attempted to kill him.

Engaged Holiness

First, St. Francis. Let me start out with another book that had a tremendous effect on me— and as far as I can tell, I am the only person who has

ever read it. I have mentioned this book repeatedly and I cannot find
another single human being who has ever read it. It was written forty or
fifty years ago by Arthur Oaken, an economist, and its title is *Equality
and Efficiency—The Big Trade Off.* The book taught me the fundamental things about economics that are still basically true. What I learned
from the book is that, if you want the economic system that is going to
produce the most stuff, that system is also going to produce the greatest inequalities of distribution. If you want equality of distribution, that
system is going to produce the least stuff. You don't have to think about
it very long to see why that's true. The best way to illustrate it is with the
leaky bucket. Let's say I take $10 from one group and give it to another
group. But when I get to the other group I don't have $10 anymore. You
know, it's a leaky bucket. So the whole time I was carrying this $10 to
the second group, money was disappearing. This is called government.
When I get to the second group, if I have a good program, I may have $6
to distribute. If it's a really bad program, it might be $2. So whenever we
redistribute we do it with a leaky bucket. That means those systems that
create the greatest equality create the least stuff.

So what do we do? Well, we compromise. We don't accept a system
that says we want the greatest possible efficiency so we're not going
to redistribute wealth at all. Nor do we say we want absolute equality,
because the leaky bucket winds up punishing everybody, since it reduces
the size of the pie so that everybody's worse off. Equality and efficiency—
the big tradeoff.

Now what does any of that have to do with Francis? We not only
think that way about economics, we have generally in Christian history
thought that way about the concepts of holiness and relevance. Those
groups that have most emphasized holiness have often been the least
engaged or relevant in the world. They throw up the walls, protect the
fort, and are not going to let you in. If I am one of those folks, then I protect my children. I protect myself. I protect my stuff. I protect my church.
Because once I start getting out there in the world, then holiness is just

going to slink away. That protection theme is in Scripture. I'm thinking particularly of 1 John, "Do not love the world and don't be of the world."

On the other hand, those groups that have often been most engaged or relevant have struggled a great deal with maintaining their identity of holiness. They become so much engaged in the world that it gets a little hard to tell the difference between the world and them. I think that's the problem in the Book of Revelation. The problem is not that the church is being persecuted. The problem is the church has become so much like the world that it is not worth persecuting and the writer of Revelation is calling the church to a radical lifestyle that will very likely get it persecuted.

So what we do then is the big tradeoff. We try to be pretty holy and somewhat engaged in the world so, like this equality efficiency thing, we say, we want 70 percent efficient and 30 percent equal or we want 50–50. I want to be holy and I want to be engaged so I'm going to do 50–50.

I want to argue that is all wrong. What you wind up with is doing both badly. It's like combining a Jehovah's Witness with a Unitarian Universalist. You get somebody who goes from door to door but doesn't really have anything to say.

All that to get to one of my heroes, a truly weird Christian, St. Francis of Assisi. I mean this guy is weird. He comes from a family of privilege, he gets involved in the crusades and has a religious experience, and basically decides to dump it all and become a totally impoverished itinerate preacher. St. Francis becomes a hero to all those who love animals and who argue for a simpler lifestyle. Somebody sent me a picture that I really cherish. It's a picture of a statue of St. Francis standing out front of a multi-million dollar mansion.

But I think Francis got this right. What I'm really talking about is the Francis-Claire tradition. Let's give the women their due. There is no Francis tradition without Claire. They're basically working together. Let me tell you about the depth of their engagement. One of my favorite stories has to do with Claire, not Francis. Claire and her group of nuns gather up some cloth and sell it so they could make a contribution to the lepers. They go to the lepers, and are bathing a leper and his skin is falling off into the water; and then they drink the water in order to have communion with the leper. Off the wall. I tell you the story not just to gross you out, but also to indicate the level of engagement that we're talking about.

If you only know one line from St. Francis, this is probably the line you know: "Go everywhere preaching the gospel and when necessary use words." So here I think is St. Francis' great idea. You lead with a radical life. Nobody can argue that Francis was not radically holy. Holy in Scripture means separate. It's not about moral purity to start out with, it's about separateness. It's about being set apart and Francis is set apart! I mean, he is not seduced by wealth, he is not seduced by fame, he is not seduced by anything. He's just plodding around from town to town preaching the gospel. He lives this radical life and people listen to him and everybody except the religious people love him. He wasn't universally loved by religious people any more than he would be today. Because anybody who lives a life that radical, even without saying anything, calls all of our lives into question. And we don't care for that. We often want to accuse such people of being judgmental, whether they are or not. How are you being judgmental? Well, you're living your life that way. Knock it off!

It's like the students in my class. They're always giving the poor smart nerd in the class a hard time because he's ruining the curve. Knock it off! You're making the rest of us look bad. But I think Francis proves to us that it is possible to live a radically holy life and be totally and deeply engaged in the world at the same time. What I want to argue is this is not 50/50. This is a 100/100. Absolutely holy and absolutely engaged. The problem is we want to call people to a holy life before we first engage them at the level that St. Francis does. One of the aspects of holiness that we seldom talk about is absolutely unconditional love, because that really sets you apart. When you do that it is possible to hold this incredibly high standard and not have people complain about it because you've already shown them that you will do absolutely anything for them.

Authentic Followship

We now hear the very hip, modern term authenticity, but Francis got there first. He understood that if you are going to call people to a radically holy life, you had better be willing to lay down your life for them. When you do that then you can make that call with authenticity. Our problem with the world is not that we have been too holy. The problem is that we have been deeply inauthentic. People don't resent holiness; what they resent is inauthenticity. I'm not saying this is easy, but I would really like to see what would happen if we took Francis' approach and lived a radical life of following Jesus Christ unapologetically and laid down our lives for people. I would just like to see for a while what results that might get. I think Francis has a really good idea here. Go everywhere preaching the gospel and when necessary use words. That is, we lead with our lives.

In a place far away there was a preacher who was struggling with his church. I just described every church in America. His elders thought that perhaps through some spiritual direction I could help out a little bit. So he and I were having a conversation. He's a brilliant guy and a capable leader. I was listening as perceptively as I could. After a while I said, "I need to ask you the million dollar question, and I want you to think about it long and hard before you give me an answer—we'll sit here however long we have to. Do you want to lead this church or do you want to lay down your life for it?" After a moment he said, "I want to lead this church." And in that moment, I knew there was no hope. Do we want to lead people or do we want to lay down our lives for them? When we lead by laying down our lives, then people might actually get interested in where we are going.

Let me suggest a modern book that very few people are reading, Scott Bessenecker's recent book, *How to Inherit the Earth*. The first chapters are worth the price. He deconstructs the notion of Christian leadership as something that Jesus is profoundly uninterested in. He starts out by going to Amazon.com and seeing how many books have the word *leadership* in them, and you get about 29,000 hits. He then checks to see how many have the word *follow* in them and you get about a thousand,

and most of these are how to lead so people will follow. There aren't any books about following. Then you go to the Gospels and you see how many times that it talks about leadership. Very few times. And when they do talk about leadership, the Gospels are almost always negative. "Don't lead like." And then you go to the Gospels and you find the concept of "following" occurs four times as many times as leading, and it's almost always positive.

We need to think about that. And I think Francis understood this. This is not about leading, this is about radical following. And when you follow Jesus into the world, then you might actually get the opportunity to lead somebody to Jesus Christ. There was nobody who was more engaged in the world than Francis of Assisi, and there was no one who had higher standards of holiness at the same time. This is not impossible. This can be done. It doesn't have to be 50/50. It can be 100/100. It is not impossible to have lives of radical holiness that are deeply engaged in the world at the same time. Francis shows us it's not impossible.

God Works in the Dark

Great idea number two. St. John of the Cross was one of the great poets of his generation and, in my opinion, the greatest spiritual director who ever lived. To read John of the Cross is to have surgery done on your soul. If you're only familiar with one phrase from John of the Cross the phrase you are probably familiar with is "the dark night of the soul." This is a truly great idea, one that we desperately need these days. Before I attempt to explain it let me put it in other words. St. John teaches that God works in the darkness as well as the light. In this day of triumphal evangelicalism, we desperately need this idea. In fact, John says God does some of his best work in the dark.

I went through a period in my life when I thought I was losing my faith. The classic symptoms were there. I was bored with the Bible. I had read it all my life. I knew it backwards and forwards. Prayer was a hopeless drudgery to me. I prayed because I thought I should, but I didn't really love to pray, and nothing really seemed to get done by prayer. I've said this

often enough—all the people I pray for die. I was preaching every week at
a church, and I hope you will understand when I say I was tired of church.
I mean, it was work to get there. The singing was like, "Where do we get
these songs?" And you know the people were hopelessly cheerful. I mean,
it was just a burden to go to church. And I was pretty bored with everything else in my life too. A person without spiritual sensibilities would
quickly see that I was in what is often called a mid-life crisis.

But St. John knows better. He describes it as "the dark night of the
soul," which is a horribly unpleasant experience which shouldn't be confused with bad. It's not a bad experience, it's an unpleasant experience.
John says, for most of us, we reach a point in life when God wants to
have a deeper relationship than he's had with us up to this point, and he
needs us to move. This is basic learning theory. You do not move until
you get dissatisfied with where you are. God in his graciousness creates
a desert around us, not to punish us, but to say, "Come on, take another
step towards me. And so as you become increasingly discontent with
reading the Bible and saying your prayers and going to church, there's
something on the other side of that—a deep relationship with God that
transcends all of that stuff you do.

A Theology of Failure

I will confess that what's on the other side of that is wonderful. I wonder
how many people out there are going through the dark night of the soul
and no one is telling them what they're going through. As I do spiritual
direction with people, the most common problem that I have is with
their concept of God. They think that when God is present that the sick
always get well, they find a parking place every time they need one, and
their church and spiritual life are flourishing. When things don't work
that way, their only possible interpretation is Job's interpretation, that
God must have fled the field on them. Instead, they should ask what it is
that God might be saying or doing or working in this darkness.

I feel as if my life has gone a lot better than most people's. I've had a
major failure or two. My failure to complete my PhD before my advisor

died is a cataclysmic failure in my profession, and God worked in that. You think I'm an obnoxious jackass now, just imagine if I had that degree. I had a mother die before she should, and a stepmother die also, but there's a lot of people whose lives have more darkness in them than mine.

In every life that mixture of darkness and light is different, but John's great idea was that we need to embrace how God works in all of it. We need to ask a different question. The question is not, "Why did this happen to me?" The questions are, "What might God do in this? How can I become more the person of God than I was? What lies on the other side of this?"

One of my covenant partners has begun to do some reflecting on the theology of entitlement that we have. We feel as if we're entitled to a certain marriage and a certain church and a certain degree of health. We just claim all that as if we had some inherent right to it. But faith means loving God when you give up all notions of entitlement. Faith is what's left. You just start peeling it all away. Again, in Job I guess the question would be, Does Job love God for nothing? Can we love God and embrace God when all of those things start to fall away? So I am really grateful for John of the Cross. I think in a real way he saved my life. I'm sorry I didn't have somebody telling me that, but again I'm an academic. I have an advantage. I read. And John just starts picking me apart and I come to understand that this is not about losing my love for God. This is learning to be loved by God and loving God better. As Thomas Merton says, this is like looking off the edge of a cliff and God saying come on, one more step, come on, come on . . . and then taking the dive.

Saying Yes to God

Which brings me to Soren Kierkegaard, who is easily the most unlikeable of the people I'm talking about in this chapter, and I can't even explain the person in a satisfactory fashion. He lives in the mid nineteenth century. He's in Denmark. There's a state church. The most important autobiographical information on Kierkegaard is that he was engaged to be married to a woman and at the last moment he backed out of the engagement, and a lot of explanations have been given for that. Kierkegaard offers a few of his own. Some have suggested that he was gay and got scared. I think there is some evidence for that, but his interpretation of it is a theological one—that he was called to do something else, and he developed a whole theology around that experience.

For him the most important story in the Bible is the story of Abraham and Isaac, where God says to Abraham I want you to sacrifice the promise that I've given to you, not just the kid, but the promise— you're going to kill the promise. Abraham's been watching the promise ride a bicycle, play on the swing set, dig in the dirt, and God says I want you to take the promise and I want you to nail it with a knife. I want you to kill the promise. Can you do that for me? That's an unnerving story, and more unnerving still is Abraham says yes. I'd love to have heard the conversation he had with Sarah over that one! "Me and the boy are going on a camping trip." I wonder what he told her. I've got some feelings for Sarah. I know she's got her problems, but Abraham gets all the messages and then he gives them to her. Does that seem right to you? I mean, what do you do, your husband comes to you and says, "God has said we are going to move." "Where?" "I don't know. He just said move."

So here goes Abraham and Isaac, and Kierkegaard's interpretation of this story is that there is a time in all of our lives when God hits us with something to which there are only two possible responses: yes or no. And in that moment we find out if we are truly going to be a follower of Jesus or not. I teach a course on the integration of psychology and theology. I'm the theology part and so I've learned all sorts of different therapies. It's really interesting when you teach a course like that. Almost everybody in there is a trained therapist. They're just finishing up their training and you know no one is paying attention to the content; they're just analyzing your process the whole time. I find strategic therapy quite interesting, and I use it all the time on my students. They'll say, "I'm going to *try* to do something." I say don't bother. You're going to fail. Don't even start. You're going to fail. There are only two choices here. Do it or don't do it. Those are the choices. You try to do it and you fail.

Kierkegaard says there comes that point of either/or, yes/no, obedience or disobedience, when you find out whether you're a follower of Jesus Christ or not. Now there's a lot of things in Kierkegaard that I think are wrong, and this choice is not a fully adequate explanation of what the Christian life is. It is a very good idea, because it is no great credit to me that I do many things that God wants me to do because I would like to do them anyway. That happens a lot. It just so happens that most of the things God wants me to do are things that I'm prone to anyway. The real test comes when God asks me to do something that I am dead set against, and then I have to say yes or no. That yes or no means more than all those other yeses which were just basically doing what I was prone to do anyway. Kierkegaard has got an idea here. There is a moment of decision.

Steps to Humility

Finally, good old St. Benedict. Benedict basically laid down the rule for all monastic life and pretty much every monastery that operates today operates under the rule of St. Benedict modified in one way or the other. And it is a fascinating rule. I reread it every now and again as I try to understand how to do life. My favorite part of the rule of St. Benedict is his twelve steps to humility. His great idea is that humility is a good idea and a very countercultural idea. Humility has got to be our least favorite virtue and, of course, it's notoriously difficult. I want to pursue humility. That's not going to go well. How humble do you want to be? I want to be the humblest person in the world! It's like teaching that impossible parable of the guys praying, you know, be merciful to me a sinner. I'm glad I'm not like him and the moral of the story is, aren't you glad you're not like that guy who said I'm glad I'm not like him. You catch yourself coming and going in that.

So Benedict's path to humility is, I think, a masterpiece of misdirection. Humility is what happens as you do other things. It's like happiness is what happens while you're doing some other stuff. You look up and discover you're happy. You know, the one way not to be happy is to relentlessly pursue happiness.

I've adapted his twelve steps to humility because if you don't adapt them, they're bad. For example, he says avoid all humor. So I'm going to present you with an adaptation of Benedict's twelve steps of humility really quick.

Number one: remember that God sees all we do—and there is something deeply humbling about knowing that God always has his eye on you. Once I was giving a lecture on the theology of Robert P. Scharlemann and just as I was starting the talk, Robert P. Scharlemann walked in the back door. As you're trying to live your life before God, God's always stepping in the back door. That puts it in perspective, doesn't it?

Number two: live by "not my will but your will be done." It is the fundamental act of submission. Jesus' praying begins and ends with submission. Both the Lord's Prayer and the prayer of the garden have that line, "Not my will but yours be done."

Number three: practice obedience. There's something very humbling about being obedient, especially when you're being obedient to people who are stupid. One of the things I try to teach my students when they're in a loser class (and even at the university where I teach there's a loser class or two) is that those classes are training in obedience. You can get something out of this and it may not have anything to do with quadratic equations. It's learning to be obedient.

Number four: embrace suffering. Very few things are more humbling than suffering.

Number five: confess one's sins. Again, very difficult not to be humbled if you're having to lay your life open before others.

Number six: be content in every circumstance. When Paul says, "I can do all things through Christ who gives me strength," what he's talking about is the ability to be content in all circumstances. I've actually done that in another way for my students. I've reduced it to two words: "quit whining."

Number seven: be convinced in our hearts that we are of no great significance. It's one thing to say it. It's another thing to believe it. To believe that if you disappeared no great hole would be left. One of the reasons why I have incorporated humor into much of my work is that I want to convey as clearly as I can that I take what I'm talking about with great seriousness, but I do not take myself with much seriousness at all.

Number eight: submit to trusted guides, living and dead, in spiritual matters. What Benedict really talks about is submitting to your abbot, but what I want to talk about is finding guides that we can trust, both living and dead, and learning how to submit to them. A group of young men I'm working with now are trying very hard to learn the process of mutual submission.

Number nine: practice silence. Silence is humbling because words are the way that we use to convey the image of ourselves that we want people to see. When you give up words, you're pretty much defenseless.

Number ten: beware of too much humor, especially the cruel kind, which avoids ever being serious. One of the things my group of committed guys tried to do one week is to speak only what love required. If love didn't require us to say it, they wouldn't say it. They would just be quiet. So if somebody really needed to talk, they would talk but they would not speak out of anything but love. They came back to report and a guy raises his hand and says, "I'm a really bad person." What we discovered is that one of the primary ways that we communicated with each other in our group was by cutting sarcasm, which among nineteen-year-old guys is often an act of great affection. But the more we thought about it, we wondered if that was the only way we want to communicate. Is the primary gift of our group in language the gift of sarcasm? Is that what we want? So I want to find out if it's possible to be serious and be a little careful with the humor.

Number eleven (notice how many of these are about speech): make your words count.

Number twelve: let your demeanor radiate humility. I think about this last one as trying to be a hospitable presence. Does my presence welcome you in or does it push you away? Humble people are not intimidating. I occasionally do get those students and others who say I just find you very intimidating. There are very few things you could say that

I find more painful, because that is a fundamental failure to display the demeanor of humility where you would be comfortable coming into my presence.

I think Benedict had a great idea. I would love to be in churches and in a world where we were cultivating humility. It boggles my mind to think about it. What would a world full of humble people look like? I try to think about it, but it's impossible.

Chapter Eleven

GREAT IDEAS FROM LIVING OFF-THE-WALL CHRISTIANS

I n the last chapter, I focused on some off-the-wall dead Christians. In this chapter I present some off-the-wall living Christians, focusing on what I think are four of the most interesting things going on in the Christian world, and especially American Christianity, right now.

The New Monasticism

The first good idea is what has come to be called the new monasticism. The new monasticism is one of the most vibrant, exciting things that has happened in American Christianity in a long time. These strange people are introducing a new monasticism. Instead of monasticism out in the desert, out in the middle of nowhere, this is monasticism planted in the middle of the inner city. There are twelve features of this new monasticism.

Number one: relocation to abandoned places. That is, new monastics are planting themselves in places that, by and large, the churches abandoned. After many churches have moved to the better neighbor-hoods, these men and women move right into the middle of those largely abandoned neighborhoods and plant themselves in the hard places.

Number two: sharing economic resources with fellow community members and the needy. I had the great honor of working with a new monastic community in Abilene called Alalone, which is a Greek reflex-ive pronoun which means "one another." I call them the wild boys. These guys moved into a house in the worst neighborhood in Abilene, which is not New York City, but it's still not good. They do not allow possessive pronouns in their language. It's not my car or my truck; it's the red car and the white truck, because they hold all things in common. They've opened a joint bank account and make all of their financial decisions together. They feed people all the time. They practice this incredible hos-pitality. They wear each other's clothes, which is distressing. They don't have internet. They don't have a television. They live very simply, so that they have more and more stuff to share with their neighbors. And they're gracious enough not only to share with their neighbors, but to allow their neighbors to share with them, which is not always easy. They had a woman in the neighborhood who was on WIC—a welfare program— who had more milk than she needed, and she brought some by to them because she thought they might need it. I am delighted to say that those young men had the good grace to accept it. They talk about the richness of this life, and I know it hits us all wrong, but it sounds a little like the early church in Acts.

Number three: hospitality to strangers. Josh, one of the Alalone guys, got a wrong number call. Instead of just hanging up, Josh talked to the guy and before long he had invited him to dinner. You go into their house and there are people all over the place all the time. One of the nights I was over there, two little kids knock on the door. The Alalone guy who answers the door says, "Anybody know those kids?" And the others said, "No." And they said, "Invite them in." They come in and they're just hang-ing around and nothing's happening. It's all boring. You know, nothing's really going on. These two kids have practically moved into the house now. For a long time I just couldn't figure it out. Why would these kids want to live where nothing is happening? But one of the guys in the house offers this explanation: Jesus is here. That's as good an explanation as I know for why they keep coming back. It's a house where the doors are open and hospitality is always offered, and I'm trying to learn more about hospitality. I'm pretty good with hospitality. I'm just not so good with the hospitality to strangers part.

Number four: lament for racial divisions within the church and our communities, combined with an active pursuit of a just reconciliation. These guys are four very white guys living in a mostly African American neighborhood. For a while there was a lot of suspicion. Some people thought they were police spies. I thought, "Well, how stupid could the police be. If I was going to send a spy in, these are not the guys I'd pick." One of the things I love best about these guys is when they talk about their neighborhood and their neighbors they don't talk about them as a project, they talk about them as their friends and their neighbors— people they decided to do life with. That attitude has the possibility of breaking down barriers that separate us.

Number five: humble submission to Christ's body, the church. It is unfortunate that a lot of people who live this sort of life seem to have a lot of anger towards the church. One of the features of the new monastics is they don't plant churches, they join churches. They believe that you need to be in submission to the church, which I think is a really great idea.

Number six: intentional formation in the way of Christ and the rule of community. Basically they're arguing for a monastic formative process. You pray together. You accept a rule of life. In the next chapter, I'll be talking about my own efforts to form a Christian community. I want to emphasize the point that you can't just assume that spiritual formation is going to happen. You have to be intentional about it. Sometimes in our churches we think that people are going to be formed by osmosis or something; but if you're not intentional about taking actions that will help people be formed, then there's no reason to think that it's going to happen.

Number seven: nurturing common life. That is, you share things together.

Number eight: support for celibate singles alongside monogamous married couples and their children. That is, in the old monastic communities everybody was single and celibate, but the new monastic communities are looking for families, married couples, and singles to be all involved in this community. I think that's a pretty healthy thing too. You're probably aware that in America today about 50 percent of the population is single. Churches that are totally devoted to families and not to singles have lost their minds. I'm going to say that as straight as I can. You cut yourself off from half the population and we just can't afford to do that.

Number nine: geographical proximity to community members who share a common rule of life. That is, the members live close together. I'm not totally convinced that's the only way to do this, but I do want to say just a word about it. The idea of the neighborhood church is not the worst idea that we ever had. It's really hard for a church to have an impact on a community when none of the members of that church live in the community. I often feel these pangs of guilt as I drive past thirty-eight churches to get to the one I attend in Abilene. There is something to be said for going back to the notion of the little community church. I think the loss of this idea is a significant loss.

Number ten: care for the earth. That is, we're going to try not to destroy the world we live in.

Number eleven: peacemaking in the midst of violence. What more can be said about the need for a peacemaking ministry?

Number twelve: commitment to a disciplined, contemplative life. That is, a life of prayer and silence and solitude.

One of the unfortunate things that has happened is spirituality movements today have split in two directions. In one direction are those who are extremely concerned about social justice, and so they're very engaged in the world. In the other direction are those who are very committed to a deeper spiritual life, and they're very committed to the contemplative life and prayer. These dimensions must be brought together. Social justice without contemplation is very likely to turn into the worst of do-gooderism, and contemplation without action is very likely to turn into a self-absorbed agnostic spirituality that doesn't take seriously our presence in the world.

If you want to know more about the new monasticism, you can read *The Irresistible Revolution* by Shane Claiborne or the book from which the previous list comes, *School(s) for Conversion: 12 Marks of a New Monasticism*. I think you'll find it really challenging. More and more young people are interested in this. They like a challenge. No offense intended, but they're bored at church, and they're looking for a way to invest some energy in a way that changes things. Observing the four Alalone guys in their neighborhood for a few months, I see that the kingdom has come in significant ways to that neighborhood. They've made some headway that I would not have thought was possible, and I am deeply convicted by it.

Now many of you are like me—you're at a place in life where you're not quite ready to do that. I think these guys are doing some praying that maybe I'll be called into that life with them (and stranger things have happened), but God is going to have to scream. But I think I have found significant ways to support and nurture their work. I want to suggest that if you're not called to join a new monastic community, maybe you're called to help those who are. You really could do significant things in supporting those who do feel called into that life.

Simple Church

The second really exciting thing I think is going on is what I would call organic church models. These are efforts to go back to what some call incarnational missional communities. In some cases they're house churches. In some cases they're cell-based approaches. But they don't have all of the trappings and mechanisms of the churches with which we are most familiar. This is sometimes described as "simple church." After you have done complicated church for a while, you have this yearning for simple. If you are like me, you may be asking yourself every once in a while how this got so complicated. You have these Christians out there trying to follow Jesus and they find each other and so they form this little community, and the next thing you know we're having deacons' meetings. How did that happen? How did this get so complicated?

I was at one of those churches that spent a couple of years working on our mission and vision statement, and I'm thinking, "How did this get so complicated?" I have gotten increasingly frustrated with this process. Once I and another minister were talking about it in the car. We drive up behind a truck with this bumper sticker. I'm not cursing; I'm just quoting the bumper sticker. It said, "Damn Good Locksmith." And he looks at me and I look at him and I know we're thinking the same thing. Now there's a mission statement. I wonder who would come to a church with the mission statement Damn Good Church. That might create outreach like we'd never had before. We'd have a whole group of people that would start to take us seriously that hadn't before.

And of course, we all experience the difficulty of trying to manage a variety of tastes on public worship and opinions about what women may and may not do, and it just gets so complicated. You start thinking about how differently that would look if it were eight people in a living room and eight more over here in this living room. It doesn't matter how well you do institutional church, 80 percent of the people out there are not going to be interested no matter how you do it. The statistics on that are quite clear. That 80 percent of the people—it's not that they're all just totally disinterested, it's just that church doesn't do it for them. But if they have a neighbor who does life with them then there are possibilities for engagement with the kingdom of God that would never take place otherwise.

Now again, not all of us are going to be called to do simple church. I'm hoping that some of us are, and I'm hoping the rest of us will support those who are called to do that. I hope those of you who are church leaders are not going to be threatened by that prospect. We've said for years that, if you are generous with your money, God will bless you. I don't know if we believe that, but if we do, why wouldn't we believe that's true of people as well? If you're generous with your people, God will bless you. If you send out people, then God will send you other people to send out. But some churches hoard people like they hoard money. You know, we're selfish with our people. These organic churches are not threats to the established church; they're just another model that's going to reach people that our current model is not. And we ought to embrace that.

I strongly recommend to you *The Tangible Kingdom: Creating Incarnational Community*, by Halter and Smay. It is a genuinely provocative book. They are a little angrier at the established church than they need to be, but you can get past that. They ask hard questions like, "Why would a church have a softball team?" If you want to play softball why don't you go join the company softball team and play softball with some pagans? Why do churches have aerobics programs? If you want to go do aerobics, why don't you go down to the YMCA and do aerobics with some people who need to see a kingdom witness? Why don't you go out there and do life with people who need to see the kingdom of God? I would also suggest Alan Hirsch's book. *The Forgotten Ways: Reactivating the Missional Church,* which is a powerful argument for a new model of church.

Many of you are like me. We have only really experienced a variation on one model of church. But we do have some younger people among us whose imaginations aren't quite so cramped, and we need to encourage them to let their imaginations go. Shane Claiborne has blessed the church with these two ideas. He says you should think about Jesus and then you should use your imagination. And when you start to think about how you follow Jesus and you do that in imaginative ways, then all sorts of interesting things happen.

I'm not totally disinterested in older models of church. But I do think the new models are one of the more interesting ideas that have come along. Of course, this is not exactly a new idea, but a rediscovery of the old idea, because that's the way the church started in the first place, if I'm reading the documents correctly.

Praying Differently

The third good idea is what I would call new prayer initiatives. There is a renewed interest in the contemplative life, and I think this has significant possibilities. One of my favorite recent books is *Punk Monk* by these guys in England who have a prayer renewal thing going among young people. These are the guys who are driving the 24/7 prayer movement. They have young people praying around the clock. Now prayer is not a new idea. What we have here is a renewal in interest combined with the notion that we don't just need to pray more, we need to pray differently.

I'm trying to get the group of guys I'm working with to think about prayer in some other ways than trying to get God to do what we want him to do. A whole lot of our prayer life is dedicated to trying to get God to manipulate the world for us. What if Martians came down and judged what you thought was important by listening to you pray? They would decide that we thought physical health was the single most important thing in the world. I wonder what happens if prayer becomes less about speaking and more about listening? If prayer is not so much a way of trying to manipulate God but about trying to get in tune with what God is trying to do in the world? That's what these listening prayer movements are seeking. After all, 24/7 prayer movements only make sense if you're in the listening prayer mode, because who's got twenty-four hours' worth of stuff to talk about?

Discernment of God's calling can only be done in solitude and silence in prayer. There has to be space for God to come in and the Spirit to move and consensus to evolve. Discernment is not just about tallying up the pluses and minuses; that's strategic planning. Discernment is paying attention to God, and that requires time and attention. One of the things I've asked my little group to do is spend at least fifteen minutes a day in silence. This is not Buddhist silence; this is Christian silence, because Buddhists believe that silence is empty and Christians believe that silence is full. There's a fundamental difference in the two. And it's the Habakkuk silence: "the Lord is in his holy temple, let all the earth be silent before him." I do not believe we can be spiritually healthy until we learn to be quiet.

Finally, in our world we are starting to get just a little bit of kickback from our obsession with constant stimulation. Now it's not enough yet. We are on the brink of disaster here. You cannot be connected twenty-four hours a day and have any kind of spiritual life. The tradition is clear about that. It can't be done. You say maybe every once in a while we should simply turn things off. The single most frustrating thing about being a teacher today (and that's saying something because there are several) is there's almost never a moment when I have a student's undivided attention. They have been trained to be constantly doing several things at once. Well, that's not so bad when they're dealing with me, but when you're dealing with God it just doesn't work well. You know at some point God's got to have your attention. So we have this growing movement of people talking about the contemplative life and practicing listening prayer. If you ever go to a monastery, as I do, it's getting where you have to have your reservations a few months ahead. I ask myself: What kind of world is this when monasteries are filling up? I think there's a bunch of people going to monasteries who aren't religious. They are people who are simply desperate for some quiet in our incredibly noisy, chaotic world.

We have great opportunities here in the life of silence and solitude and prayer. I hope we'll find a way to feed that. One of the major things that church leaders would want to do is to think about how we can help our people live saner, quieter, more prayerful lives. But what we often do in is pile more stuff on top of their already chaotic lives and make them slightly crazier than they were before. That's not what God calls us to. He calls us to peace.

The Opportunities of Postmodernity

The fourth thing that I think is interesting and promising is what I could call the postmodern critique. Churches of Christ, like other Christian traditions, were deeply formed by the assumptions of the modern age. Many of those assumptions have to do with human ability to create the complete set of answers to the complete set of questions. We may not know the answer yet, but give us some time, let us develop the tools, and we'll come up with the answers. So a great enemy of modernity would be the concept of mystery. Mysteries ought not to be a permanent part of our lives. They should be things that we attempt to overcome and solve. It's like a mystery novel. By the end you want to know who did it.

I think those assumptions are really hard on both spiritual life and church life. A whole series of writers from a variety of standpoints have started to raise questions about modernity. A really fine book by a writer who comes out of the radical orthodoxy tradition is *Who's Afraid of Postmodernism?* His basic argument is that, far from having anything to fear from the postmodern move, postmodernity raises great opportunities for Christianity.

For example, what if we come to the conclusion that science isn't going to be the answer to all of our problems? I think the evidence is beginning to mount up. Science has delivered a lot, but its' not going to be able to deliver everything. Better political theory is not going to solve all of our problems and I think the evidence might be mounting up on that one too. Sociology and psychology may not be able to solve all of the problems that afflict us. I teach a course on the integration of psychology and theology. I'm not a disdainer of psychology. It has taught me a great deal. I'm serious about sociology. I like sociological research, although they are often researching stuff that I don't find very interesting. But social and psychological engineering just aren't going to solve all our problems.

When you come to the conclusion that those avenues essentially aren't going to be able to deliver what they promise, then it's possible to start talking again about how to live in a world without all the answers. I think biblical religion at its best is a discussion about how you do that, how you live with hope, how you live with faith, in the face of a world that you cannot fully understand or control. What if you came to the conclusion that truth could be found not just at the end of a syllogism, but in the experience of the divine? What if religious experience becomes a way of knowing again, as it was through much of the two thousand year history of Christianity?

I'd like to relieve some of your anxiety about the passing away of the modern world. It could be chaotic, but in the midst of that chaos there are ripe possibilities for a new breakout of biblical religion, that is, religion driven, not by the complete set of answers to the complete set of questions, but by the genuine experience of a living God. There is more openness to that possibility than at any time in the last hundred years.

There is the possibility for a new great awakening upon us, because if you've hung out with any young people at all, you know that they're pretty driven by experience. In fact, they are so driven by experience that they frighten me. I had a conversation with some students the other day. We were having a disagreement in my office and I was brilliantly supplying them evidence that a position they were defending was wrong. They weren't quite buying it yet, and I just said, "Tell me how much evidence it will take and I will produce it. I will bury you in evidence. I will pile it up to your neck. I will fill the room with it. I will make it absolutely impossible for any right thinking person to deny my position on the issue at hand. I have no doubt I can do that." And guess what? Evidence didn't matter to them. That's a little frightening.

On the other hand, their openness to an experience raises all sorts of possibility for the living God. In Acts 10, with one little experience, God wrecks Peter's life. And there's that possibility (if you're paying attention and you're open to it) that God can come in and do things. So it's going to be a little rowdy, but I'm fairly excited about the dawning of the postmodern world. I'm not a particularly optimistic person. Optimism has always seemed to me to be an odd way to go at things. You know, it just creates all sorts of disappointment and makes you fairly obnoxious to those around you who are realists. But I think there are a lot of reasons to be hopeful about what can happen. The places where Christianity is doing best in the world at the moment are places where modernism is most in the background. And the places where Christianity is doing worse at the moment are the places where the dominant paradigm is a modern one—in Europe and the United States. We are fretting over what will happen to us if we give up the notion of truth and certainty.

Well, I think we have to hold on to truth. But certainty has always been overrated. Maybe it's not going to be so bad.

Those are four good ideas. The new monasticism, organic church models, new prayer initiatives, and the postmodern critique. In the next chapter I will talk about my favorite contemporary thinker and strange Christian. Me.

Chapter Twelve

GREAT IDEAS FROM ANOTHER OFF-THE-WALL CHRISTIAN

W e have looked at good ideas from off-the-wall dead Christians and good ideas from off-the-wall living Christians. In this chapter, I will give what I think are my own good ideas. I don't think I have to argue that I am an off-the-wall Christian (my students can testify to that), but I will argue for the goodness of these ideas. And as with the other ideas we have looked at, they are not really new but rediscoveries of some old good ideas.

Risk

Great idea number one: take a risk. Do something beyond your comfortable resources. It's always easier to play it safe. My favorite definition of following Christ and Christianity comes from a guy named Maltbe who said, "Jesus promised his disciples three things—that they would be completely fearless, absurdly happy, and in constant trouble." The problem is we are seldom in trouble and that makes it very difficult for us to be either happy or fearless because to be those things you have to be in trouble. So we play it too safe and are so far behind the enemy lines that the notion of reliance on God becomes relatively unimportant, because for the most part we do not need him. Now, despite what you see, I do have areas of competence, and I'm telling you, when I am functioning in those areas I am largely unaware of God. Because I know what I'm doing and I know how to do it. I am most keenly aware of God when I get out in those areas where I'm not nearly as comfortable and knowledgeable about what I'm doing.

I was struck again as I was reading this story of the feeding of the five thousand in Mark. It's a story about the resourcefulness of Jesus. All these people haven't shown a lot of foresight; there's only one kid who thought to bring a lunch and Jesus takes his! The apostles tell Jesus, "We got lots of people out here. It's getting dinner time. You need to send them off to eat." and Jesus says, "You feed them." I mean, they're being practical. Jesus is being ridiculous. They find this kid's lunch and it turns out to be enough. ,

I'm just not convinced we have a resource problem. I think we may have a faith problem. I think I have to believe that God provides all of the resources to do the stuff that he's called us to do. The problem is most of it's in our pocket and I'm not just talking about financial risk; I'm talking about taking spiritual risks. Putting yourself out there beyond your spiritual comfort zone. I'm talking about ministry risk where you start something you're not entirely sure you can finish. I'm talking about bringing some excitement and adventure back to life, and not always living comfortably within our own resources. I had been planning for five years to launch my little religious order, but I continued to talk myself out of it because I knew I wasn't ready. Finally, one of my friends says, "You're going to be dead before you're ready. Just do it. Quit waiting to get ready, just do it and trust that God will provide you the resources you need. And if he doesn't, then you'll fail and we'll all enjoy watching that." I thought that was great advice. If you believe God's on the throne, then you're as free to fail as you are to succeed because God works through your failures as well as he does your successes.

Walk

Number two: walk. This is to say, move at the speed of God which is much slower than we usually move. It's really interesting in the Bible that almost all the important stuff that happens in Jesus' life with the disciples happens while they're walking. The people who have written about pilgrimage and walking, they've really gotten me thinking about this. We do have to think about what kind of walking we're talking about here. I'm not talking about your power walking. I do that too. Generally when I'm home (if there's no good reason not to) I walk four miles a day by myself. I cultivate doing it by myself by wearing my ear reduction headphones with my little cord in my pocket attached to nothing. I do not want to listen to anything,

That's not what I'm talking about. I'm talking about the other kind of walking. Now one of the things that astute observers have noticed is that when you are driving, everyone else who is driving is your adversary. Driving is essentially an adversarial relationship, and it is really hard to develop relationships as you drive. There is no universal hand signal for "God bless you." There are very few things you can communicate to others while you're driving—and they're almost all negative. But when you're walking, everybody else is walking and it's a kind of companionship. I decided to try something different. Whenever I have a meeting somewhere on campus to which I must walk, I'm going to leave ten minutes early and meander. I'm going to say, "God, give me two or three students on the way." Lo and behold I have a wonderful two- or three-minute conversation with students on the way. And I'm walking across campus and here are these students slack lining. You know what slack lining is? It's where you tie this line up between two trees and you get on top and walk on it. They said, "Come on over and slack line with us." So I throw off my shoes and a guy gets on either side of me and I start slacklining.

So there's something to this walking thing. It's moving at the speed of God which is always slower than we think it is. God likes slow. All you have to do is read the Bible. God likes slow. Ask Abraham and Sarah. God likes slow. You know, I've pointed out to my students that one of the difficult things about dealing with God is that, if Scripture is believed, he has no sense of time. You know what it's like to deal with a human being like that. Here's Abraham and Sarah saying, "God, we're getting up into our hundreds. I mean we're getting too old to go to soccer games." And God says, "Oh! I'm sorry. I was just having a cup of coffee. I hadn't noticed. Let me get back to you." God likes slow.

My friend Mark describes this as making room for divine interruption, that is, not tying your life up so tight that it's not possible for people to interrupt you. I really have tried to have more flex in my schedule because when a student really needs to talk to me, I don't need to tell him I have time for you a week from today. I've taken this so seriously that a friend of mine and I have walked to church a couple of Sundays, and it's just the most wonderful experience. I first drove over to his house so we start at the same place, and it's about a four and a half mile walk. It takes us an hour or so; and, boy, that was a sweet hour; nothing to do but walk and talk and get stared at by people driving to church. Often the most important ministry you do is while you're on your way to what you think is the important ministry. If we just kind of slow down and that can happen.

Move

Number three: relocate. Now I'm not telling you to move across country. I'm just telling you to be where light is needed. Relocate to the places where people need to see light. As we started our little group, one of the things I tried to convey to them is that your life cannot revolve around this group. We want you to be out there, and we want you to pick the places where you want to plant yourself on this campus to be salt and light. For some of us, this is just hard. I mean we've gotten so comfortable on the inside, we don't know how to function on the outside. We all need to find places where we're going to rub shoulders with people who need some light.

Now for some of us, it may mean actually moving, changing our place of abode or location. I don't want to try to talk you out of that if God's trying to talk you into it. But short of that, we have to be some places where sinners are.

Calm

Number four: be calm, prayerful, and sane in the midst of craziness. We're just coming off of the craziest possible time at a university—April. My former department chair would say, "We do not accept any resignations in April; otherwise we would not have a faculty." It really would be profound witness if Christians would be the calmest, sanest, least crazy people in the world. I really do long for that time. I spend a good bit of my life in airports. It's hard to tell the Christians from the non-Christians in an airport. As I struggle to figure out what the next phase in my life should be, the one part I'm sure about is that it's time to get quieter. It's time to talk less. It's time to listen more. It's time to calm down. It's time to quit looking as crazy as everybody else does. Too often in our churches we ask people to come in and trade their form of craziness for ours. You were driven when you came in and now you'll be driven about some other stuff, rather than letting that drivenness go. I spent a little time at a Buddhist retreat center. Basically I was just trying to learn to sit. I wasn't planning on becoming a Buddhist. It's just that if you want to know how to sit, they're the best sitters in the world. I'm serious about that.

My goal was, if my plane was going to be two hours late, to be able to sit in the airport without a book and be perfectly calm and all right with that. For you it might mean, if your doctor is forty-five minutes late for your appointment, instead of thinking about all the things you could be doing with that forty-five minutes, you're sitting calmly and prayerfully and openly before God, thinking "Isn't this wonderful that I've got this forty-five minutes given to me that I hadn't planned in my day "And that would improve your life.

That's why I went to the Buddhist monastery. It was great. They were very hospitable. It was an unnerving situation because I'm a Christian and this was not a Christian environment. But that taught me a lot. I was feeling very Zen-ish when I left. I had spent some afternoons picking cherries, working on the wood pile, and working in the garden and I was just exceedingly peaceful. I wondered how long my Zen would last, and I got home and it carried on. I decided to let the spiders continue to occupy my abode with me. I generally had killed spiders, but I decided no, I'm going to let them live here. Then on a fateful morning I get out of bed, walk into my bedroom closet and there curled on the floor is a snake, and I lost my Zen. It didn't help that he was a little aggressive, although I admit if someone were trying to kill me with a tennis racket I might be aggressive too. I initiated hostilities. I might as well admit it. And I thought it didn't take much to lose my serenity.

Prayerful, calm, sane. I actually think Scripture has a word that tries to convey all of this in one word. The word is that wonderful Hebrew word *shalom*. It means being at peace with God and at peace with yourself and at peace with your surroundings. We experience this well-being as we know that God is on the throne. I think we ought to cultivate that.

Simplify

Number five: simplify. What I'm talking about primarily here is material simplicity. I think that most of us still live lives that are materially extravagant. We're much richer than we think we are. I took inventory the other day and, you know, I'm absolutely convinced I could get rid of 20 percent of my stuff with zero sacrifice. That would only improve my life and it would cost me nothing. I could get rid of 20 percent before I even started to feel it. The only thing I would notice is I've got more room. Then I can start thinking about how to simplify my life some more.

Those guys in the intentional community Alalone have shown me a lot about the richness of living simply. I want to simplify my living some more so I have more to give away because I have found that giving stuff away is one of the most fun things in the world to do. I love giving things away and I don't think I've simplified my life enough yet. Now there is no way to talk about this without it being guilt inducing. If you saw the way I lived, you would know I'm a long ways from having this figured out. I just want to tell you that in this area guilt is not such a bad thing. Maybe we should feel guilty because we are. Shame is the work of the devil; you have to watch out for that one. But guilt is a gift of God as we come to recognize that we're not living into the values that we claim.

Commit

Number six: commit. I was recently reading the book by Shane Claiborne and John Perkins, *Follow Me to Freedom: Leading as an Ordinary Radical*, a glorious mess of a book. It doesn't ever quite become a coherent whole but there's wonderful stuff on almost every page. You probably recognize John Perkins as one of the really great heroes of the Civil Rights movement. He was almost murdered in Mississippi years ago. At one point, the young Claiborne is complaining about how slowly the work is going in Philadelphia, to which the older Perkins chimes in gently, "Well, you got to wait ten years because it takes ten years to do anything substantial."

Now that is hard teaching to a whole generation that has become ADD. We have churches and Christians who have the attention span of gnats. We flip from one thing to another without ever making the deep commitments that it takes to achieve anything of lasting significance. Again, my friends at Church of the Savior have this famous line for which I am the poster child. They say, "If you're overextended you're under committed," and in some ways that's a definition of my life. I've got my hand in so many things that I'm not deeply enough committed to any of them, and if I had it all to do over again I would commit more to less. I would try to find those things that I want to give my life to and stick with them. In this world of instant gratification this is very counter cultural; it's going to be difficult because we like results and we like them pretty quick. The folks at the Church of the Savior say it makes a much bigger difference if you do small things consistently over time than if you do big things and then abandon them. We easily overreach and burn ourselves out and back away from ministries; and there's little evidence a short time later that we were ever there at all. So I challenge you to do some reflection on what is worth your energy for the next ten years or so. What is it you want to give your life to?

Present

Number seven (and this is the easiest one and the hardest one): be present where you are. Don't live in the past. Don't live in the future. Be present where you are. The present is God's time of working. Douglas Steere said, "The greatest impediment to a genuine experience of God is the fleeting remembrance of our last experience of God." There is that tendency to live in the past, but there's also the tendency to live in the future. I try to convey to my students that you're not preparing for life, you're living it. You know, there's nothing more real about working an eight to five job than there is being a student. They have exactly the same reality, and if you're always thinking about a future moment you're failing to live in the present moment.

I'm really impressed with Jesus on this. He seems to do this extraordinarily well. He's present with people, and so he can have encounters with people that take mere moments, but in those moments it's as if he and that person are the only two people in the world. This is one of the primary goals of my life—to convey to the person in front of me that, though I may be doing something else five minutes from now, right now I'm with you. I'm there with my heart. I'm there with my mind. I'm there with my attention. When a student comes into my office, I don't want to be answering the telephone. I want to be paying attention to that person. I wish I did this better than I do, but I just keep reminding myself through the day to tend to what's in front of me. I cannot tell you how much happier that makes me.

There's a psychologist who has given me four statements that I really hold dear. He says if you can't say these four things uncommonly often, your life it not going very well. "There's no place else I'd rather be. There's nothing else I'd rather be doing. There's no one else I'd rather be with."

And fourth, "I will remember this moment." If you can't say those four things uncommonly often, he says, then life probably isn't going very well.

Well, this is about as close as a theologian can come to doing something practical. The kingdom of God is not a theory. It must be tangible. We've got to live out of an experience and bear witness to the reign of God in the world in practical, everyday ways. My guess is if we didn't do anything else the rest of our lives other than that, at the end we would say that was good. That's what I meant to do with my life.

Chapter Thirteen

PRACTICING PEACE

W e live in a world that is deeply driven by anxiety and fear, and it brings our personal lives and our world to the brink of disaster. So in this chapter I want to offer some reasonably deep reflection on what the life of peace with God would be. I begin with expressions of inward peace, and want to talk about practices that actually make peace operational in our lives.

Holy Indifference

The first practice is holy indifference. Now when we use the word indifference we're almost always using it in a negative way. How can we get people to quit being so indifferent? But a substantial part of Scripture is encouraging us to learn to be indifferent, because the truth of the matter is that most things we worry about don't matter, and finding peace is largely learning to be relatively indifferent to those things. Now if you think I'm just making this up, let me go to the Sermon on the Mount and share a passage on indifference. That's not the word that's used, but that's what Jesus means. Matthew 6:25–34:

> Therefore I tell you do not worry about your life, what you
> will eat or drink or about your body what you will wear. Is not

life more important than food and the body more important
than clothes? Look at the birds of the air, they do not sow or
reap or store away in barns and yet your heavenly father feeds
them. Are you not much more valuable than they? Who of
you by worrying can add a single hour to his life? And why do
you worry about clothes? See how the lilies of the field grow.
They do not labor or spin yet I tell you that not even Solomon
in all his splendor was dressed like one of these. Yet that is
how God clothes the grass of the field which is here today and
tomorrow is thrown to the fire. Will he not much more clothe
you? Oh you of little faith. So do not worry, saying, 'What
shall we eat? What shall we wear?' for the pagans run after all
these things and your heavenly Father knows that you need
them. But seek first his kingdom and his righteousness and
all these things will be given to you as well. Therefore do not
worry about tomorrow for tomorrow will worry about itself.
Each day has enough trouble of its own.

If you come to believe in the ultimate trustworthiness of God then
you can start to put worry behind you. The key to being able to stop worrying is to put most things in life in the category of "relatively indifferent"
and some things in the category of "doesn't matter at all." I think we can
choose to assign things to those categories.

I occasionally get into a conflict with a student about a grade. And
so I try this on them. I say, "Look. Do you really think anybody is going
to care ten thousand years from now whether you got a C+ or a B- in my
class? I don't think anybody will care a hundred years from now. I don't
think anybody will care ten years from now. I don't think anybody but
you (and perhaps your parents if a scholarship is at stake) will care next
week." And they usually think about it and say, "I couldn't agree with
you more. Why don't you give me the higher grade if it doesn't make any
difference?" Think about the amount of emotional energy we put into
things that are relatively indifferent.

I want to suggest an attitude towards most things in the world: bemused. This word should become part of your vocabulary. We should learn to be bemused as opposed to angry. If you can learn to be bemused, life gets much easier. You know that in ten thousand years it's not going to matter so let's let it go now. One can choose to develop that kind of attitude towards life.

In one of my advanced preaching classes I had a student whose preaching style was to pound us relentlessly for twenty minutes. The problem is when you pound everything we hear nothing. And when everything in the world becomes the most important thing in the world, then the really important things aren't important anymore.

Like many of you, I struggle with worry about material things. I have tried to develop this practice of not having anything that I'm afraid to have broken. When I invite students to my house I often invite them into my kitchen first thing and I pick up a mug and drop it on the floor and break it and tell them there's absolutely nothing in this house that I care about more than I care you. So make yourself at home and if you break something it really doesn't make any difference. We can all relax. I had one student who shortly after that broke my coffee table. He tested my holy indifference. Well, I passed. I think I passed. When you buy a new car the first thing you should do is get a hammer put the first dent in it yourself. That way you do not have to park at the end of Wal-Mart. You can park close because you've already got a dent in it. Great idea. It's liberating. There are some areas of life where we need a little less indifference than we have, but in most areas of life we need a lot more indifference.

I visit different churches almost every week and, boy, they're worried about some stuff they ought to be bemused by. They are just absolutely worrying themselves to death over stuff that they ought to be relatively indifferent to. Now this doesn't have to do with not caring, it has to do with caring passionately about stuff you should care about. My old (dead) friend, Augustine, (says sin essentially amounts to loving the wrong things to the wrong degree, and there's a lot of wisdom in that. Things are to be used not loved. People are to be loved not used. We easily get those two things confused—we wind up loving things and using people rather than loving people and using things. If we can develop the attitude of holy indifference it then becomes possible to start to live into the reality of "do not worry," because the number of things that are worth worrying about suddenly goes way down.

Peaceful Rhythm

Second, in the practice of peace we need rhythm. We need a rhythm of life that makes sense. My evidence for this is Jesus. In Luke 4, 5, and 6, Jesus goes off for prolonged times alone with God in prayer. Luke 4:40ff: "When the sun was setting the people brought to Jesus all who had various kinds of sickness, and laying his hands on each one he healed them. Moreover, demons came out of many people shouting, 'You are the son of God," but he rebuked them and would not allow them to speak because they knew he was the Christ. At daybreak Jesus went out to a solitary place. The people were looking for him and when they came to where he was they tried to keep him from leaving them, but he said, "I must preach the good news of the kingdom of God to the other towns also, because that's why I was sent. And he kept on preaching in the synagogues of Judea." Luke 5:15–16: "And the news about him spread all the more, so that crowds of people came to hear him and to be healed of their sicknesses. But Jesus often withdrew to lonely places and prayed." And finally Luke 6:12ff: "One of those days, Jesus went out to a mountainside to pray and spent the night praying to God. When morning came he called his disciples to him and chose twelve of them whom he also designated apostles."

Three times in a row. This is a really meaningful pattern. It's the pattern of Jesus' life. He's alone with God. He's out ministering. He's alone with God. He's out ministering. And it is this rhythm of life I think that allows Jesus to do what he does without getting frantic. I don't know what you're having to deal with in your church, but I'm telling you that the twelve were no bargain and he's having to deal with them constantly. He's got the crowds around him, and there are times when Jesus says enough is enough. Off he goes to be with God. In that Luke 5 passage it even says he walks away from hurting, needy people in order to pray. By the way, if you are going to pray that is the only way you are ever going to do it, because if you wait until you get all of the hurts healed you will never pray, because there's always one more person who needs you.

We have developed preachers and church leaders who are totally arrhythmic in their life. We need this rhythm of solitude and prayer, and our failure to do that is largely what has made us frantic and anxious. It is part of our anxiety that we think that prayer always means talking. Every once in a while I'll have student in my office talking about something and I say, "You know, I think we just need to pray over this." They'll bow their head and I'll bow mine and we'll just sit. They're wondering, "Did he die or stroke out? When are we going to start to pray?" Well that's what I'm doing. And then they get the idea. Prayer has always primarily been a way of listening. I tell preachers that I really believe that silence and solitude is the only remedy for the compulsiveness that drives most of our ministry, because in silence and solitude you once and forever give up control.

Eugene Peterson talks about the rhythm of Genesis 1. Evening, morning, day one. Evening, morning, day two. And he says that rhythm is no accident. The ancient view was that at night God takes care of things while you sleep and then in the daytime you do your part and take over. Now think about that. When is the world in better hands? The world is never safer than when you're asleep! We do not believe that and the rhythm of our lives proves it. We act as if everything depends on our next action and so we live this frantic, driven life that creates anxiety in us and the people all around us. It is a failure to trust God who works in all things. So in addition to holy indifference, we need a better rhythm of life.

Grace-Infused Graciousness

The third characteristic is grace-infused graciousness. Paul Tillich's description of grace is something like the following: the courage to accept one's self as accepted, even though you are unacceptable. As definitions of grace go, that is better than "unmerited favor." That kind of gets to the heart of what graciousness is. We understand ourselves as accepted by God even though we are unacceptable.

Now if you look carefully there are several parts to that. There is a big problem if you do not know that you are unacceptable, and that leads to all sorts of horrible things. In Jesus' words when you've done everything you can do, you are still an unprofitable servant. So if we can make peace with being unacceptable, we don't have to try to convince anybody that that's not the case. The other part of that is, even though I am unacceptable, God has accepted me. When I come to believe that, then that infusion of grace empowers me to be gracious to others in the same way, and that starts to bring peace on the earth.

I was talking to one of my good friends not long ago about some struggles with a mutual friend, and I said, "You know, he's just a little bit difficult." And then we got to talking about another friend and it turns out we were both struggling with him, too. And I said, "Well, you know he's a little bit difficult, too." And then I looked at my friend in front of me, and I said, "In fact, you're just a little bit difficult." And I came to this incredible insight about the world. Everybody in the world but me is a little bit difficult. And the ability to accept one's self as accepted even though you're unacceptable admits, first of all, that I'm a little bit difficult. And when I admit I'm a little bit difficult, it allows me to be a little more gracious to everybody else out there who's a little bit difficult.

I want you to let your mind roam and think about the person or group of people that you have the hardest time extending grace towards. I don't even have to think about it. For me, it's child abusers. I, like many of you, deal with their messes and it's the gift that keeps on giving. It's like it has no end. I can feel my blood pressure rising just thinking about it. But I pause for a moment and tell myself that nobody comes out of the womb saying that what I really want to do with my life is be a child abuser. I have a friend on the police force in Abilene. He actually did a degree in our department and then became a policeman. He does it with a deep sense of calling and mission. So I was riding with him one night just to see what Abilene after dark is like. They stopped this guy who had a warrant out and he had a teenage nephew with him, probably fourteen years old. They got the guy out of the car, cuffed him, then called a relative to come and get the nephew. What was striking to me is how calm the boy is. Here he is, this relative he's been riding around in the truck with is being arrested, hauled off to jail, he's standing out here on the side of the road with this policeman and he's taking it all in stride. I'm sitting there thinking what must it be like to live in a world that is so chaotic that this is just same old regular stuff.

I grew up relatively poor, and my parents were far from perfect, but I've come to appreciate how much stability there was in my house. I always knew I was loved. I always knew home was a safe place, that no one was likely to be arrested that night. It was a stable environment and I just keep wondering if you take me out of my environment and drop me into this kid's environment, how does that turn out? I don't know What I do know is that, having all the advantages in the world, I still conduct a life whereby I am unacceptable and that God still accepts me. I'm hoping that I can learn to be a little more gracious to those other unacceptables out there (which would constitute pretty much everybody).

Now I'm not trying to confuse villain and victim. Let me assure you I know the difference. But the world will not be made worse off because we are too gracious. I wish I were the person that some of you think I am, but I know I'm not. When I preach or teach, there are several people who really know me, and to just listen to me requires enormous graciousness on their part because they know I don't live up to the message that I preach. And if they can be that gracious to me, can I extend that same graciousness to other people?

Now what does that have to do with peace? Well, if you can accept yourself as accepted even though you're unacceptable, first of all, you start to get some real interior peace. And second, if you can extend that same graciousness to other people, then I assure you much deeper peace is going to break out. It can't help but do that. Now my feeling is if you try to do these three things, holy indifference, the rhythm of Jesus, and grace infused graciousness, if you try to do these things without being grounded in your identity in Christ, it's not going to work. First of all, you have to get your theology right. You have to know that your identity is found in Christ and your security is found in God. Because you're a member of the kingdom of God and the kingdom of God is never in trouble.

Imagining Peace

Pause for a moment and exercise your imagination. Think about what would happen if you became relatively indifferent to all the things in your life and church that really don't matter. Use your imagination. Consider what life would look like if you didn't think everything hinged on your next action. Think about what life would be like if you really believed that God loves you so much that there's nothing that you could ever do that would make him love you more or less—that his love is absolutely relentless and that the divine love could become the love that you have for other people. If you want to talk about revolution and transformation in the world, it is just that simple (not to be confused with easy because there's nothing easy about it).

I keep calling people back to the Sermon on the Mount where Jesus says the wise person is the one who hears these things and puts them into practice. Jesus believes that not only should you live this life, you can live it. And it is the most practical, world-transforming way to live you can imagine. Dietrich Bonhoeffer writes words that are very close to the following: If there is going to be a new restoration in our time it will be because of a new monasticism that has in common with the old monasticism only this one thing: the seriousness with which it takes the Sermon on the Mount. And the notion that by simply living into these instructions of Jesus we can transform the world I think is the single most important interpretative move we make regarding this Sermon.

Chapter Fourteen

PEACE AT LAST

Sometimes in our theology we have tended to emphasize the destination as if the trip didn't matter. But most of the Bible is not about the destination, it's about the trip. This business of peace is not about so much going to heaven, it's about what we're doing on our way there because the trip is very, very important.

Inside Out, Outside In

There is a really interesting study of arranged and non-arranged marriages in India. And as you can imagine, those who had chosen their own partners scored higher in passion or love than those with arranged marriages. Obviously if you get to choose your own partner you're going to be more madly in love with them. That's not the interesting part. The interesting part is what happened when they gave those same couples that same test twenty years later. Those in arranged marriages now had a higher level of passion and love than those who had chosen their partners. Let's stop and ponder that for a while.

I really do believe that this practice of peace is inside out. You have to develop certain attitudes and perspectives and ways of dealing with the world and then behavior flows out of that. But there's another side of me that sides with this arranged marriage thing where if you start behaving in a certain way then you begin to get it. That is, you fall in love with the concepts and the ideas as you're practicing them, so it's not just inside out, it's also outside in; it's not just the destination, it's also the trip—but it's not just the trip, it's both the trip and the destination.

Wheat and Weeds

How does this peace move from peace with God within myself to a more peaceful world? The first thing we need to do is quit assuming that the world is full of weeds and instead work from the assumption of wheat. Matthew 13:24ff:

> Jesus told them another parable. "The kingdom of Heaven is like a man who sewed good seed in his field, though while everyone was sleeping his enemy came and sewed weeds among the wheat and went away. When the wheat sprouted and formed heads then the weeds also appeared. The owner's servants came to him and said, 'Sir didn't you sew good seed in your field. Where then did the weeds come from?' 'An enemy did this,' he replied. The servants asked him, 'Do you want us to go and pull them up?' 'No,' he answered. 'Because while you are pulling the weeds you may root up the wheat with them. Let them both grow together until the harvest. At that time I will tell the harvesters first collect the weeds and tie them in bundles to be burned then gather the wheat and bring it into my barn.'"

I hope you haven't gotten so familiar with the Bible that this story doesn't strike you as being at least a little odd. Jesus seems to be looking at the world and these harvesters, saying we know there's wheat out there but there are also weeds. Do you want us to try to get rid of the weeds? And he says no because weeds and wheat look an awful lot alike and you're incompetent to separate them. Jesus says no, let them grow together and in the fullness of time God will sort it out.

That is a recipe for creating deep peace in our world because generally we work with the assumption that you are a weed and then wait for you to prove that you're wheat, rather than assuming that you're wheat and waiting for God to see that you are a weed. We judge too quickly and we judge wrongly. Jesus is basically saying you're not entirely competent to do this, so maybe you just better wait and let me do it.

We simply aren't discerning enough to pick out weeds from wheat; but the way we have decided to solve that problem is by assuming everything is a weed. Wrong impulse. Jesus says let's do that the other way. You treat it like wheat and if it's a weed I will take care of it in good time. Think about what a difference it would make to the hostility in our world if we worked with the assumption of wheat instead of weeds. In other words, if we gave people the benefit of the doubt.

As I've taught college students I've found this out more and more. Everybody wants to tell students what they're doing wrong. That's a significant part of my job, to correct their thinking and help them think better. But I've noticed over and over again how transformative it is when I treat them not like a weed but like wheat. That word of blessing, that word of encouragement, that giving the benefit of the doubt becomes transformative to them. Not only that, it keeps me from making some terrible mistakes because, as Jesus points out, we judge too early and our measurements just aren't that good.

What I'm basically doing is echoing Jesus and saying let's quit being quite so judgmental. Let's act as if we live in a world of wheat and leave it to God to sort out the weeds.

Beyond Us and Them

Number two: let's quit thinking about the world in us/them terms and see people altogether differently. 2 Corinthians 5:11ff: "For Christ's love compels us. Because we are convinced that one died for all and therefore all died. And he died for all that those who live should no longer live for themselves but for him who died for them and was raised again.

Paul talks about this redeeming work of God and now here's the so what:

> So from now on we regard no one from a worldly point of view. Though we once regarded Christ in this way, we do so no longer. Therefore, if anyone is in Christ, he is a new creation. The old is gone. The new has come. All this is from God who reconciled to himself through Christ and gave us the ministry of reconciliation that God was reconciling the world to himself in Christ, not counting men's sins against them, and he has committed to us the message of reconciliation. We are therefore Christ's ambassadors. As though God were making his appeal through us, we implore you on Christ's behalf be reconciled to God. God made him who had no sin to be sin for us so that in him we might become the righteousness of God.

We no longer see the world in terms of us/them; we see the world in terms of reconciled and not yet reconciled. This is a very different way of looking at the world. What does it mean that, after we look at the world through the cross of Christ, we no longer see anyone from a worldly point of view? When I see you from a worldly point of view I'm trying to size you up. I'm trying to decide what kind of prospect you are. But when I see you through the redeeming work of Christ, I see you only one way, as one for whom Christ died. In that regard, we are always the same. We are both people for whom Christ dared to die. One of us may be more reconciled to God than the other, but it's not us/them because what we share is Christ's death for both of us.

Everything in the world pushes me to see the world in terms of us/them. In our political parties it's us/them. In our world conflicts it's us/them. Whenever anybody uses the pronoun "we," my ears perk up because I want to know who "we" are, as opposed to "them."

We're conditioned to think in terms of us/them; and the ministry of reconciliation keeps pounding on the door and says no, no, no, this is not us/them. Christ died for all. And so we no longer see anyone from a worldly point of view, though we used to do that. Now we see each other in a completely different way. Christ came to bring about reconciliation.

Crossing Boundaries

I know it's probably not possible to get entirely rid of us/them thinking. I try to pay attention to it in my own language and it is true that churches are communities with boundaries. That is, if they're worth anything. They have boundaries; and everything good that has been accomplished in the kingdom of God for the last two thousand years has been accomplished by communities that have identifiable boundaries. This is the complicated part. So there is a sense in which there are those who are members of this group and those who aren't still, I think it is possible to live out of that reality without us/them thinking being our primary mode of operation. That is, the boundaries are rather porous—we're always looking for others to come in, and we're always wandering out. We're not going to think about the world primarily in terms of us/them.

At the end of the Sermon on the Mount when Jesus talks about loving enemies, if I understand it correctly, he is trying to get us to break out of that us/them thinking. Remember the particularity of the language: when you love people of your own clan or tribe, that makes you exactly like every other pagan in the world. Everybody loves like that. What marks you as a follower of Jesus Christ is your ability to break out of that tribalism, that us/them thinking, and include more people in your world of prayer and grace. And so sure there may be categories out there, but that's not the way I think about the world anymore. The way I think about the world is, Christ died for all and what we have in common is more important than anything that's trying to drive us apart. If we want peace in the world, let's start thinking about the world in a different way because the world's tribalism is bringing us to the brink of utter disaster.

The Cross Story

Number three: let's look at the world from the point of view of cruciformity. We have to look at the world through the story of the cross and
resurrection, as opposed to all the other stories the world is giving us.
It's very hard to resist the story that the world is trying to place upon us.
We easily accept the world's story; we just accept a better form of it. If
you're a man, the world tells you that your worth is determined mostly
by how successful you are in making money. And if you're a woman,
the world tells you that your worth is based on your ability to acquire a
certain look. Of course, we're way too sophisticated for that. We are not
falling for that. People's worth is not based on their earning ability and
not on their looks. Why do we make the claim that value is not based on
appearance and then want to make sure that you know all our children
are above average and good looking? Why is it when it comes to hiring
and firing preachers, we say their worth is based on how successful they
are with success measures taken almost entirely from the world—how
many and how much—and we don't even notice that we're still embrac-
ing the world's story?

What the story of cross and resurrection asks us to do is not to
accept the world's story —even if we soften it somewhat. What it asks
us to do is embrace a radically different story about worth, success, and
what makes life worth living. What are the implications of calling Lord
someone who was crucified and that God raised up? What are the implications of letting that story be your story? The most profound implica-
tion of that story is that I don't have to worry about protecting myself or
to exert power or live in fear because God's got me. I can lay down my
life before others because, even if you kill me, I won't stay dead. It radically sets me free to be generous and self-giving, because now I know my
security doesn't depend on me anyway.

Now I've got a reason to get up in the morning. It's not just the destination, it's the trip. And so I have this story that I want to live. I want
to be cruciform in all things. I want to be cruciformed in how I treat my
students. I want my students to understand I don't just have the grade

book; I have an obligation from almighty God to find ways to lay down my life before them. I want that cruciformity to spread into all areas of my life, and I want to do it as a happy warrior.

I'm not an optimist. I don't even understand optimists; to me, optimists are people who just don't understand the situation. Optimism depends on human beings and I don't see much reason to be optimistic. But I'm very hopeful because hope is hinged on God, and I see every reason to be hopeful. The resurrection says these things we do for the sake of the kingdom of God, the little ways we lay down our lives, every cruciformed act, ripples through eternity and that sets me free to live in self-giving ways I never could otherwise. If all Christians would do this simple thing—live out the story we claim we believe, the story of cross and resurrection—we would experience peace in our world in ways that we have never experienced before.

Peace at last.

Soul Work

*Confessions of a
Part-Time Monk*

Sharing experiences and insights from his visits to monasteries over the years, popular speaker Randy Harris invites us into a richer, fuller life in the Spirit.

Most of us don't have time to visit a monastery for a week or a month. So Randy Harris shows how the monastery can come to you. With wisdom, humor, and captivating insight, he guides you on an unforgettable journey. You will learn prayer, humility, surrender, and quietness along this well-traveled path.

156 pages $13.99   ISBN 978-0-89112-272-2

LEAFWOOD
PUBLISHERS

An imprint of Abilene Christian University Press

www.leafwoodpublishers.com

1-877-816-4455 toll free

God Work

*Confessions of a
Standup Theologian*

Can theology be practical? Entertaining?
Relevant? Anyone who has heard Randy
Harris speak will answer with a resounding,
"Yes!"

Combining his experience as a professor of theology with a popular style
that makes the profound understandable, Harris opens us up to the world
as God intends.

*"I've seen Randy in front of thousands.
No one is better: no one articulates
deep, rich, Christ-centered words any
better. But I've also witnessed him with
one or two students: laughing, praying,
encouraging, challenging, befriending.
Randy is one of the few people about
whom I can say, paraphrasing Paul,
"Follow his example, as he follows the
example of Christ."*

—**Mike Cope**,
Pepperdine University

163 pages $13.99   ISBN 978-0-89112-628-7

An imprint of Abilene Christian University Press
www.leafwoodpublishers.com
1-877-816-4455 toll free

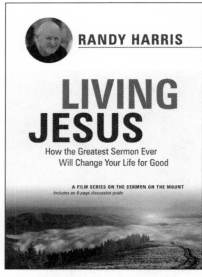
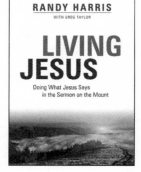
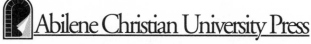